Better Homes and Gardens®

Favorite Houseplants
--and how to grow them

Cover photo—*Various green and variegated foliages surround two African violets (Butterfly White and Lavender Fluff). All of these plants make ideal candidates for terrariums.*

Back cover—*Grow a passion flower vine for dramatic blooms in summer and fall.*

Right—*Begonias, with their near endless variations of flowers and leaves, offer continual indoor beauty.*

Better Homes and Gardens Books

Editorial Director: Don Dooley   Executive Editor: Gerald Knox
Art Director: John Berg   Production and Copy Chief: Lawrence D. Clayton
Assistant Art Director: Randall Yontz
Garden and Outdoor Living Editor: Beverly Garrett
Garden Book Editor: Steven E. Coulter   Landscape Editor: Russell O'Harra
Associate Garden Editor: CarolAnn Shindelar
Graphic Designers: Harijs Priekulis, Faith Berven, Sheryl Veenschoten
Consultants: Hamilton Mason, Dr. L. C. Grove

Contents

A thriving collection of indoor plants

Keep your houseplants happy

Houseplants don't exist in nature. Most of the species cultivated today once grew wild on some part of the earth—in rain forests, deserts, moist woodlands, or arid prairies. As indoor plants, they've been uprooted from their preferred climates and forced to adjust to completely new conditions. When put in containers, plants are cut off from normal root development—they can't send down deep root systems to seek life-giving water and nutrients. Indoors, rains can't reach plants to furnish needed moisture and to clean foliage.

So, the more you know about your plants, their native habitats, and the growing conditions they prefer, the better. That's where this book will become as indispensable as your watering can.

On the next page begins an alphabetical listing of plants, from African violets to zebra plant. Under each listing you'll find a photo of that plant, plus everything you need to know to keep it alive and thriving: facts on light, water, feeding, proper potting mixture, propagation, and trouble signs.

Following the alphabetical section, you'll find information on bulbs that you can coax into early bloom to add a touch of spring to winter, plants especially suited for growing in terrariums, plants that you can grow in water instead of soil, and how to care for holiday plants to prolong their bloom.

Next is a 12-page section called Green thumb basics—information common to all kinds of houseplant culture, such as the different amounts of water to give your plant depending on whether it's in a clay pot, a plastic pot, or a ceramic container; how to clean your plants to keep them breathing properly; what to do with your plants when you go on vacation; five ways to reproduce houseplants; and much more useful information.

At the end of the book, you'll find a glossary to help you distinguish nodes from runners from bracts. In addition, there's an index listing plants by both common and botanical names so you'll be able to find your sansevieria even if you know it only as snake plant, hemp plant, or mother-in-law tongue.

African violets (left to right): **Gay Confetti, Crown Red, Clipper, Crown Red, and Delft Imperial**

Houseplants A to Z

African violets (*Saintpaulia*). A favorite houseplant in millions of homes, the African violet isn't a violet at all—but it does come from Africa. Its popularity hinges on its free-blooming habit during the year. Single and double flowering varieties are available in blue, violet, purple, lavender, red-violet, blue-violet, pink, lavender-pink, and white. Petals may be crimped, ruffled, or frilled. Foliage may be green or variegated, with plain or wavy-edged leaves.

Light: African violets will not bloom in a room having low light intensity. If you don't get a distinct shadow cast on white paper where the plant is located, it's not getting enough light. Light from outside windows must be unhindered by trees or any outside structure. An east sun is preferred. During summer with its strong sun, a north window offers a good exposure. Reduce the intensity of direct sunlight with sheer curtains.

Bring African violets into early bloom under fluorescent grow lights. An electric timer can be set to switch on the lights and turn them off automatically after 12 to 14 hours exposure. Allow only about four inches between the light source and top of plants. When flower buds start to open, move the plants to living areas for decoration and enjoyment.

Water: Water as soon as the soil surface feels dry. Always use lukewarm water—never colder than room temperature. To prevent soil from clogging up the drainage hole, cover it when potting with a shard—a piece of a broken clay pot. If your pots don't have drainage holes to allow surplus water to drain away, be on guard against overwatering. African violet roots must never stand in water; the methane gas which forms from such a condition is very toxic to roots.

Special helps: African violets do well in a temperature range of 60 to 75° F. Avoid subjecting them to sudden changes of any kind. If temperature is too low, foliage turns pale and curls.

For regular flowering throughout the year, use one of the fertilizers specially designed for African violets. Follow the instructions on the label carefully.

The African violet is easy to propagate from leaf cuttings. Leave 1½-inch "stems" attached to medium-size leaf cuttings. Stick the stem in moist medium—sand or vermiculite—with the leaf just above the surface. Cover the cuttings by pulling a clear plastic bag down over a couple of bamboo stakes. This helps maintain proper humidity. (While leaves can be started in water, transferring the tender roots to potting soil requires special care.) Root in good light, but allow no sun to strike cuttings. Keep the rooting medium moist. In six weeks, cuttings will have rooted and can be potted up in individual 2¼-inch pots. Barely cover the roots. Often, several young plants will sprout from the base of a leaf; they should be separated and potted after three good-sized leaves have formed on each plantlet.

African violets must have a porous soil. Use a commercial potting mixture specially designed for African violets, or make your own consisting of equal parts by volume of coarse sand or perlite, rich loam soil, and peat moss or leaf mold.

If foliage looks burned, plants have received too much intense sun or too cold air. Place a sheet of aluminum foil between plant and window on very cold nights to reflect room heat back onto the plant to protect the foliage.

Leaves that touch the rim of the pot often rot at the point of contact and fall off. This is caused by the action of soluble salts that accumulate on the rim. Avoid this by dipping the rim of the pot in hot paraffin before planting, or crimp a narrow strip of foil over the edge of the pot. If white cottony mealybugs attack, kill by touching each pest with an alcohol-soaked cotton swab.

1. Leaves that touch rim of pot may rot at the point of contact.

2. White cottony mealybugs on leaves can ruin a plant.

3. Inadequate light results in long stems and few blooms.

4. Root leaves to start plants.

Agapanthus (*Agapanthus africanus;* lily-of-the-Nile). Six-inch clusters of tubular flowers will open gradually over a six-week period if you keep your agapanthus in a cool location. Do not overpot—this plant blooms best when roots crowd each other. Peter Pan and Dwarf White are good varieties for containers. Flower stems will reach two feet in height.

Light: Agapanthus likes at least half a day of full sun.

Water: Keep soil just moist from early spring to September. Let foliage be your guide. If it sags, give more water.

Special helps: In spring and summer only, feed every two weeks with any complete soluble or liquid fertilizer. After flowering, if the pot is completely rootbound, divide the clump of tuberous roots into several portions. Use any general potting mix of average fertility. Agapanthus is virtually pest-free. Old leaves yellow naturally; remove them gently.

Airplane plant (*Chlorophytum comosum;* spider plant). Although the grasslike leaves with their creamy stripes are attractive, the real appeal of this plant lies in the cascading runners that terminate in multiple plantlets. These form their own root systems which you can cut off and pot up individually.

Light: The airplane plant loves bright light. If you wish, summer it outdoors in a spot protected from damaging wind.

Water: Add water whenever surface of the soil dries out.

Special helps: Grow your airplane plant in an all-purpose potting soil. Feed mature plants three or four times a year. Let newly potted plants become established before feeding.

Aralia confusion. When shopping for Balfour aralias (opposite page), don't mistakenly buy a false aralia (Dizygotheca elegantissima), which is also called Aralia elegantissima. See page 23 for the description and culture of dizygotheca.

Agapanthus

Aralia (*Polyscias balfouriana;* Balfour aralia). Although these plants are sold as aralias, polyscias is the correct name. *P. balfouriana* is the variety shown here. Its erect stems bear shiny dark green leaves, each with three roundish leaflets two to four inches across. Variegated forms are also available: *P. balfouriana marginata* features white-edged leaves; *P. balfouriana pennockii* has slightly cupped, milky green leaves edged in dark green.

Light: Balfour aralias perform best when given four or more hours of direct sunlight daily; but they will grow well in bright indirect light. Even in locations with only man-made light, aralias survive admirably.

Water: Keep the soil barely moist. Mist the foliage to increase humidity, or place the pot on a pebble tray and keep the water level almost to the top of the pebbles.

Special helps: Feed established plants three or four times a year. Repot rootbound plants in spring, using a general all-purpose potting mixture. Propagate any time of year from stem cuttings (see page 88 for stem-cutting details).

Airplane plant

Asparagus meyeri. This relative of common *Asparagus sprengeri* and florist's asparagus "fern" produces dense plumes one to two feet high. Each stem of *A. meyeri* looks like a miniature Christmas tree, and a clump resembles a bonsai woods. Each branch is densely covered with what looks like green "needles"—actually flattened stems that serve as leaves—giving the *A. meyeri* its nickname of foxtail asparagus fern.

The Sprengeri asparagus fern has been a favorite hanging houseplant for generations. Its 18- to 24-inch-long branches are covered with bunches of inch-long, bright green needles. Another ornamental asparagus variety is *Asparagus plumosus,* the fern often added by florists to bunches of cut roses.

Light: Shelter the ornamental asparagus ferns from direct sun. Part shade or filtered light is ideal.

Water: Keep the soil moist, but not soggy wet. Needles often turn brown and drop off in the dry winter climate of most homes, so mist regularly or use pebble trays to provide additional humidity if your air is warm and dry.

Aralia

Special helps: Your main problem with *Asparagus sprengeri* will be the roots. They rise like dough, leaving no room for water after a year or so. When this happens, unpot the plant, chop the roots into halves or quarters, and repot each segment.

You can't just pull *A. meyeri* apart indiscriminately as you can *A. sprengeri*. Wash soil off the crown of the plant so you can see clearly where you're making cuts. Otherwise, you are apt to lose precious stems. After making the cuts, you can easily separate the sections. Propagate at any season.

Grow your asparagus ferns in rich, well-drained soil. A general-purpose potting mixture will suffice. Add gravel to bottom of container before you put in soil and plant. Feed three to four times yearly with houseplant fertilizer. Summer the plants outdoors in a semi-shaded area.

Asparagus meyeri

Aspidistra

Aspidistra *(Aspidistra elatior).* Commonly called cast-iron plant, aspidistra lives up to its nickname. One to two feet long, tapered, dark green or variegated leaves arise from a crown.

Light: Aspidistra tolerates a wide range of light. While it will survive in dark corners, it will be more luxuriant near windows out of direct sun.

Water: More problems arise by overwatering than under-watering. Water thoroughly, then let soil surface dry.

Special helps: Aspidistra can handle temperatures from 45 to 85° F. Solid green type prefers rich soil (two parts good garden soil, one part compost or leaf mold, one part perlite or sand), but variegated varieties change to all green in rich soil. Feed in spring and summer. Too much hot sun will yellow leaves. White spots with brown margins indicate fungus disease—remove entire leaf and burn. If fern scale insects appear (white males; brown, oyster-shaped females), wash them off with soapy water. Trim off brown leaf tips. Obtain new plants by dividing old ones. Cut roots apart with a sharp knife. Shade new transplants from direct sun.

Aucuba *(Aucuba japonica).* This dense, shrubby evergreen plant grows three feet tall in a pot—larger in a planter. Prune to keep under control and to make shrub bushier. Leaves are leathery and glossy. Gold-dust plant's nickname derives from yellowish specks on oblong-shaped foliage. Female aucubas produce small purple flowers followed by scarlet berries.

Light: Supply bright, indirect light—some east sun will do. Turn plant regularly to expose all sides to same light.

Water: The large number of leaves use lots of water, so never let soil dry completely. Mist foliage regularly.

Special helps: This cool-loving plant—60° F. is ideal—does better on an unheated porch than in a warm living room.

Use standard potting soil mixture. Feed in spring and summer. Take stem cuttings to start new plants—see page 88.

Avocado *(Persea americana).* To prevent this cost-free houseplant from getting too tall, cut at least 1½ inches off the top to induce branching. Do the same with branch tips.

Light: A sunny east window is fine, but keep plant away from direct sun of south and west exposures.

Water: Water as soon as the soil surface feels dry. The container should have good drainage to avoid root rot.

Special helps: Save a few seeds from the fruits bought for eating purposes. Wash seeds in warm water to remove clinging matter. Plant seed in potting soil with ¼ of the pointed end of seed above soil level. Or root in a glass jar or other clear container. Stick four toothpicks into sides of seed so it will rest on edge of glass. Keep water level touching broad base of seed. Position in a warm spot without direct sun. Germination is fastest at 85° F.—slower at lower temperatures. Only mature seeds will germinate. In four to eight weeks the seed will split as a tiny stem arises. Pot up carefully when well rooted.

Aucuba

Adjustment period. *Sudden or drastic changes can shock and stunt any plant. Expect withdrawal symptoms such as dormancy or leaf drop when you repot or otherwise upset a plant's normal light, water, humidity, and temperature conditions. Make these changes gradually, if possible, to give the plant time to adjust to its new environment.*

Avocado

Banana plant

A banana plant won't provide you with fresh fruit (nor will your home-grown avocado or mango), but what a tropical effect it offers. A few ornamental, reasonably small banana varieties do produce inedible fruit with honest-to-goodness seeds that are large and easy to handle. Plant the seeds as you would those of any other plant.

Banana plant (*Musa nana [cavendishii]*). Dwarf banana plant—sold as *Musa acuminata*—will reach six feet at maturity. This banana variety is not a tree, since the stem is nearly all water and has no bark. Keep this luxuriant tropical plant indoors—the large, tender leaves tear easily in the wind.

Light: The banana plant thrives on bright, indirect sun.

Water: Keep soil moist all year. Watch the leaves. They're hinged along the central rib and will fold down or turn brown if the plant isn't receiving enough water.

Special helps: Supply your banana plant with rich, porous soil. Give a light application of any completely soluble or liquid fertilizer every other month from March to September.

You'll find your banana plant virtually pest-free. Old leaves at base of stem turn yellow; cut them off with a knife or scissors. Mature plant will deteriorate after several years. Cut off at base and discard (or cut up for compost pile, if you have one). If the plant is large, you may need a saw for this task. Divide and repot the suckers that have formed underground at the base of the parent plant. (They would crowd each other if left undisturbed.) Dig down carefully, separate the sprouts, each with its roots, and pot up.

Bougainvillea (*Bougainvillea glabra; B. spectabilis*). Many named varieties of this plant are available. They are usually tall vines, but the bushier forms are easier to keep within bounds, simply by cutting them back after flowering. Bougainvilleas bloom intermittently from late winter through summer. The vines have no natural means of support, so you need to stake and tie them—being wary of the thorns.

Bougainvilleas are erratic about dropping leaves in late fall. Sometimes, they go completely bare; sometimes, only partly so. The red-purple and yellow-orange flowered types are your best bets for good bloom. The white-flowered and variegated-leaf forms are a bit difficult and shy-blooming. Variety Barbara Karst is one of the most satisfactory.

Light: Bougainvillea loves full sun; if possible, supply at least four hours of sun daily the year around.

Water: Water when soil starts to dry out. If in doubt, don't water; bougainvillea survives dryness better than excessive wetness. Be sure pot has adequate drainage.

Special helps: Bougainvillea prefers well-drained, moderately fertile soil. Apply any completely soluble or liquid house-plant fertilizer monthly from early spring through summer.

Propagate bougainvillea by taking semiwoody cuttings in late spring. This lets you obtain a number of new plants without disfiguring the original specimen. Remove a single leaf along with a bud and a piece of stem. Insert the stem section in a handful of moist sphagnum moss in a plastic bag. Tie the bag firmly around the stem of cutting and set it in a spot away from direct sun. When the roots show up inside the plastic, pot up the new plant. Other plants that can be propagated by semiwoody cuttings include rubber plant, hibiscus, and snowflake plant.

Brassaia (*Brassaia actinophylla,* also called *Schefflera actinophylla* and *S. macrostachya;* commonly called schefflera, Australian umbrella tree, Queensland umbrella tree, octopus tree). This leafy beauty requires little attention. It's available in all sizes, from eight-inch seedlings to ceiling-height trees. The rate of growth is moderate, though, so don't be alarmed by the eventual size the plant can reach. If yours gets too big, reduce its size by air layering.

The foliage boasts a natural high gloss that's easy to restore if it becomes dulled by dust. Rub gently with a soft cloth or use your thumb and index finger to renew sheen.

Light: Brassaia likes strong light, but not direct sun.

Water: Water each time the soil surface starts to dry.

Special helps: Use a general potting mixture. Feed lightly once or twice a year. Propagate by air layering (see page 89). Make a cut partway through stem at a strong angle and insert a matchstick to keep cut open. Mold a baseball-size wad of wet sphagnum moss around the cut, and enclose in a sheet of plastic. Keep moss moist until new roots form, then pot up.

Insect control. *If mealybugs attack your bougainvillea or other plants, white cottony blobs will appear on almost all parts of the plant. Dab each bug with a cotton swab dipped in rubbing alcohol.*

Fine webs along veins and leaves indicate the presence of red spider mites. Leaves will turn dull green or grayish, with stippled surfaces. To control, give the foliage a weekly bath in soapy water, or take plant outside and use a miticide, following the manufacturer's directions carefully.

Brassaia

Bougainvillea

LEAF TYPES

B. multiflora rosea

B. semperflorens

B. lucerna

B. dregei

B. heracleifolia

B. manicata

B. haageana

B. rex

B. ricinifolia

B. scandens

B. luxurians

B. semperflorens flowers

A fibrous begonia behind two rex begonias

Begonias. Of the three major categories of begonias, the rhizomatous and fibrous-rooted are grown most often as house-plants, while tuberous begonias make ideal candidates for hanging baskets on porches and patios. The best-known member of the large begonia family is the fibrous-rooted, ever-blooming group called wax begonia, with its shiny or waxy leaves. Flowers range from red and pink shades to white, and may be single or double. Grow wax begonias indoors or out. Most fibrous-rooted kinds grow about a foot tall; the popular angel-wing begonia stretches higher.

Begonias grown *primarily* for their beautiful foliage belong to the rhizomatous rex group. Hairy, textured leaves arise from their short rhizomes. Foliage color may be purple and green, silver and green, or the distinctive rich chocolate and green of the iron cross begonia. Provide filtered light for the glamorous rex begonias all year long.

Tuberous begonias rank among the showiest of flowering plants. Flowers range in size from three to eight inches in diameter, and come in double and single form with plain, ruf-fled, and frilled petals. Colors available include apricot, orange, salmon, yellow, crimson, scarlet, pink, rose, and white. Hang this trailing begonia outside for summer-long pleasure. It delights in fresh, clean air.

Light: Most begonias don't like too much sun. They do well in open shade or with some early east sun. They withstand some winter sun better than hot summer sun, which should be filtered. For the most blooms, grow wax begonias in a sunny window during the winter when sun is less intense.

Iron cross begonia

Beefsteak begonia behind two smaller foliaged begonias

Water: Keep the soil evenly moist; avoid extremes of too wet or too dry. Water as soon as soil surface feels dry. Good drainage is essential; waterlogged soil will rot roots.

Special helps: Pot up begonias in a loose soil mixture containing plenty of organic matter. Use two parts compost or other available organic matter, one part perlite or coarse sand, and one part good garden loam.

Use care in fertilizing—a slow-release type of houseplant food works best. Give a light feeding every couple of weeks when begonias are blooming.

Diseases and insects to be on guard against include bacterial leaf spot, botrytis blight, stem rot, and mealybugs. Bacterial leaf spot causes blister-like spots on the foliage. Pick infested leaves and burn them. Botrytis blight and stem rot turn plant parts brown and black. Remove infected areas and burn. If mealybugs appear, touch each pest with a cotton swab saturated with rubbing alcohol.

Propagate fibrous-rooted begonias such as wax begonias by stem cuttings. Remove the lower leaves from three- to four-inch-long cuttings and stick the stem ends in a moist rooting medium such as vermiculite or sand. Then, cover with a clear plastic bag to create a moist, greenhouse-like atmosphere. To keep the plastic from touching the foliage, which can cause rotting, insert stakes into the medium. Keep the cuttings in a warm spot out of direct sun. Allow three weeks for the cuttings to root, then pot them up.

Propagate rhizomatous begonias having leaves with large veins, such as the rex types, by leaf cuttings. Remove a leaf along with one inch of leaf stem from a mature plant. Insert the stem in a moist rooting medium. Anchor the leaf, face up, with toothpicks and sever each main vein. Cover the pot with plastic to maintain high humidity. Roots and plantlets will form at the cut points. When plantlets develop several small leaves, remove them from the parent leaf and pot up individually.

Or, cut the big leaf apart so each section includes a part of the main stem. Remove and discard the tips of each piece to reduce wilting problems during the rooting process, and insert the base of leaf sections in sand, vermiculite, or perlite. To keep the leaf piece from toppling, sink the lower third into the rooting medium. Open the medium with a knife. If you try to push the soft leaf into the medium, you'll crush and ruin it. Check for good roots after two or three weeks. Then pot up each in a two- or three-inch pot.

Start summer-flowering tuberous begonias from tubers in February or March. Set the tubers in a shallow container of loose, moist rooting medium such as vermiculite, leaving the pinkish buds exposed. When rooted, pot up in five-inch or larger pots, depending on size of the new root system.

Water sparingly at first; increase amount of water as the plants grow and can use more moisture. In fall when plants show signs of resting, gradually withhold water. When tops have died down, store tubers in dry vermiculite or sand.

Propagate big begonia leaves

1. Section leaf; remove tips.

2. Pot up sections when rooted.

3. Or, anchor leaf; sever veins.

Vacation care. *When you grow bromeliads, you don't have to worry if you go away on a trip. Just remember to fill the plants' centers or cups with water, then leave with a clear conscience. The water should last for two or three weeks. If it should all evaporate, the plants will still survive another few weeks—but don't deprive them unless you have no other choice.*

Painted feather *(Vriesia 'Mariae')* **bromeliad**

Bromeliads.
This large family of ornamentals also includes the pineapple and Spanish moss. Many of these plants have such striking foliage that they remain decorative at all times, even when not in flower—the flower spike lasts three months or more on many. Their sculptural quality provides an asset in any decor, contemporary or traditional.

Flowers of the neoregelias—one group of bromeliads—stay small and often bloom unnoticed in the water of the cups. To enjoy the blooms, move the plants to a location on a low stand or coffee table for viewing from above. The spectacular color of the foliage offers a show itself.

Other bromeliads of special interest include *Aechmea fasciata* ("urn plant"), with bluish-green stiff leaves, frosted white, and a spike of pink bracts with blue flowers; *Vriesia 'Mariae'* (painted feather), with plain green leaves, but a brilliant spike of yellow and red; *Vriesia splendens 'Major,'* 'flaming sword,' green leaves striped brown, orange spike; *Vriesia viminalis 'Rex,'* red bracts with yellow flowers, good for small spaces.

Light: Bromeliads prefer bright, but not full sun.

Water: Keep water in the center cup of the plant at all times. The root system is small. Water lightly around the base of the plant once a week. Overwatering of roots will cause the plant to rot at the base.

Special helps: Bromeliad care is easy—even in the "fool-proof" class. Feeding is optional. Plants will grow for years, content with whatever nutrients they get from the water. If you're not content without feeding, a little liquid fish emulsion (dilute according to directions and use at half strength) added to the water in the center cup should be of some benefit if applied every six to eight weeks during the summer months.

Bromeliads reproduce themselves by suckers put out from the base of the parent plant after the parent flowers and dies (this process often takes a year or more). As the parent plant dies, leaves turn brown. Simply peel them off as they loosen and become unsightly. Some kinds, such as aechmea 'Foster's Favorite,' really proliferate, with perhaps a dozen offsets. Others, such as 'flaming sword,' produce only one or two new plantlets, which appear from the center cup of the old plant.

Offsets should have short, stubby roots; pot up individually in three- or four-inch pots. Use only a porous potting soil—either shredded tree-fern bark and osmunda, or regular potting soil mixed liberally with perlite or sand. Barely cover the base of plant with potting mixture. Stake until roots develop enough to support the young plant. Water sparingly.

Neoregelia carolinae 'tricolor' bromeliad

How to propagate bromeliads

1. This aechmea will make about 12 new plants when divided.

2. Cut the offset close to the base of the parent plant.

3. Barely cover the base of the plant with porous potting soil.

Calamondin orange

Chinese evergreen
(*Aglaonema commutatum*). Although much splashier than their solid-color cousin, the variegated types are just as easy to grow.

Light: These hardy plants will grow anywhere except in direct sun. However, the variegated types need medium-to-bright light to retain their flashy leaf markings.

Water: Keep soil barely moist at all times.

Special helps: Use any all-purpose potting mixture, being sure to provide adequate drainage. Propagate by root division or by stem cuttings from excessively tall plants (see page 88).

Citrus trees.
Orange, lemon, lime, and grapefruit trees all will grow indoors in pots or tubs. Popular calamondin orange (*Citrus mitis*) doesn't grow above two feet high. (Be sure to buy established plants, as this tree is grafted onto a root stalk.)

Planting seeds from any citrus fruits will result in attractive green foliage, but flowers and fruits may not form. Start the seed in a small pot and shift it to progressively larger ones as soon as roots fill the container.

Light: Grow in a sunny window in winter, then set in sun outdoors in summer. Toughen your citrus by easing it outside gradually. Set it first where it gets a little east sun a few hours each day for a week. Expose to more sun gradually.

Water: Soak plant well when you water, then let dry before soaking again. Fruits tend to drop if plant is over- or underwatered. Citrus prefers humid air; mist foliage daily.

Special helps: Citrus does best in slightly acid soil. Use soil mixture containing an acid peat. Once a month, apply ½ teaspoon of vinegar mixed in a quart of water. Also use a slow-release plant food to give citrus the moderate fertility it needs.

Lack of pollination indoors results in no fruiting. If you want your tree to bear fruit, shake blossoming plant slightly each day to distribute pollen, or use a camel hair brush to transfer ripe pollen to sticky surface of stigmas in centers of blooms.

Clivia
(*Clivia miniata*; Kafir-lily). Exotic clusters of orange flowers generally appear in March or April. Glistening green, straplike leaves provide a foliage show the rest of the year.

Plants have to be large to bloom. At best, clivia is slow to bloom, but once started, it's dependable year after year. Root-bound plants bloom better, so don't repot often.

Light: Clivia likes bright light, but spare it from direct sun.

Water: Keep soil moist from late winter through summer. Reduce to light watering in fall through midwinter.

Special helps: Clivia thrives in rich, well-drained soil, so be sure to use ample sand or perlite. Feed lightly every two weeks from late winter through summer with any complete soluble or liquid plant food. Crown rot may attack if soil remains excessively moist. If this happens, remove whole plant from soil, dust with folpet (a fungicide), repot, and keep dry for two weeks.

Propagate by root division immediately after flowering. Expect to wait two years for divisions to start blooming.

Clivia

Chinese evergreen

Coleus (fittonia in back; see page 32)

Croton

Coleus. These foliage plants come in seemingly endless color combinations of red with green or yellow edges, and chartreuse, light and dark green, and bronze markings. Leaves display many patterns; some even sport ruffled edges. Mature plants produce spikes of insignificant blue-purple flowers.

Light: Coleus will tolerate shade, but growing them in sun will bring out their maximum range of colors.

Water: Since coleus leaves are large and thin, they give off lots of water and wilt readily unless they have access to water almost continuously. Water regularly for lush growth.

Special helps: Feed once a month with regular houseplant fertilizer. Propagate from stem cuttings (see page 88). Use a standard potting mixture. Pinch tops to induce dense growth.

Croton (*Codiaeum*). Other plants pale beside the flashy croton. The hundred-plus varieties dazzle with different leaf colorations and shapes. The one shown combines spots and streaks of green, red, pink, yellow, black, with flushes of orange.

Light: If crotons don't get strong light—even full sun—for at least four hours a day, they will turn green and lose their usual rainbow colors. Full coloration will return if you summer your plant outdoors when the sun is strong.

Water: Crotons like moist, but not wet soil at all times. They react adversely to hot, dry conditions and may drop leaves, so provide as much humidity as possible by misting daily.

Special helps: Use a general-purpose potting mixture. Feed every other month from early spring through midsummer. Air layer or take stem cuttings in spring or summer.

Dieffenbachia. Several varieties of this popular houseplant are available. One of the toughest is *Dieffenbachia amoena,* with big, bold, dramatic leaves. If you're short on space, try the small-leafed varieties such as Rudolph Roehrs (*D. picta*), which features chartreuse leaves with green midrib.

Light: Dieffenbachia tolerates a wide range of light—from poor to bright. Full sun, however, will yellow the handsome foliage. So give it north, east, or west light—but no more than two hours of direct sun a day.

Water: Don't let the soil dry out completely or the edges of the leaves will become discolored. If the leaves start to droop, you know that water is needed. One way to water thoroughly is to immerse the pot (not the plant itself) in a pail of water. When the water stops bubbling, the soil is saturated. Remove the pot and allow the excess water to drain out of the bottom of the container. If your house is dry, move your dieffenbachia into a steamy bathroom occasionally.

Special helps: This native of the tropics likes 70° to 80° F. temperatures. Use standard potting mixture. Fertilize with regular houseplant food in spring and summer.

As plant matures, lower leaves die, leaving a leggy stem that's unsightly. Cut off the plant several inches above ground

Dieffenbachia (Chinese evergreen on right; see page 21)

Dizygotheca

level and root the stem in water. After roots form, you can pot up the plant or continue to grow it in water. The original potted plant will sprout a new stem on the stub.

Or, you can renew the leggy plant by air layering. To do this, make a cut partially into the stem at an angle and insert a wooden match to keep the cut open. Wrap a baseball-size wad of wet sphagnum moss around the cut, enclose it in a sheet of plastic and tie the plastic at top and bottom. Keep the moss moist. In four weeks, the moss ball will be filled with new roots. Cut off the stem below these new roots and pot it up.

Dizygotheca (*Dizygotheca elegantissima*; false aralia; thread-leaf).

Botanically speaking, this indoor shrub, which reaches five feet tall, is a dizygotheca—but asking for it by that name wouldn't get you far in the supermarket. In ordinary trade, it remains *Aralia elegantissima*. Elegant it is, but by no means as delicate as the foliage might lead you to believe.

Light: This plant needs little light and will thrive for years with only artificial overhead light. However, a summer change does it good. Put it outdoors under a tree where sunlight is well filtered. Tie plant to a stake to avoid wind damage.

Water: Water thoroughly once every week to keep your dizygotheca in peak shape. Supply good bottom drainage. Leaf drop may result from either too dry or waterlogged soil.

Special helps: Use a standard potting soil mixture. Feed established plants lightly every two weeks only during active growth period—early spring through summer. Propagate by root division (see details on page 88).

Dumb cane. Dieffenbachia's nickname refers to the fact that the acrid sap in its leaves and stem will burn the mouth and throat and may temporarily paralyze vocal cords. When handling this plant, don't put your fingers in your mouth or rub your eyes!

Dracaena janet craig

Dracaena warnecki

Dracena (*Dracaena*). The great variety of dracenas available provide dramatic forms for interior design. These impressively large foliage plants make good choices for either formal or informal settings, regardless of whether you use them singly or as focal points for mass arrangement of plant collections. And as an added plus, they are easy to grow.

Dracaena fragrans massangeana often is called the corn plant because its wide leaves resemble those of a cornstalk. The yellow stripe that runs the length of each leaf will disappear if the plant stands too far from its light source, but the all-green foliage is still lush. Brown leaf tips indicate improper watering—either too little or too much.

Dracaena janet craig has several relatives of similar appearance, all of which often are called dragon trees. They do well in medium light and average house humidity if grown in porous soil and provided with good drainage.

The striking leaves of *Dracaena warnecki* make it popular in spite of its tendency to develop brown tips and edges. You can snip off these discolorations with scissors. Plants thrive in small pots—seemingly disproportionate to the size of the plant. Repot to a larger container only if new leaves fail to develop.

One of the most desirable of indoor plants, *Dracaena marginata* has narrow bottle-green leaves edged with red. This angular, sculptural plant will reach a height of six feet.

Dracaena godseffiana, called Florida Beauty, is a dwarf, maturing at 18 to 24 inches tall. Its wiry stems of green leaves mottled with creamy white grow in a haphazard manner.

Light: Grow in an east window or out of direct sun in south and west windows to maintain brightly colored foliage of the variegated types. Dracena will survive with only remote artificial light, but growth will be much slower.

Water: Dracenas withstand neglect for some time, but it's best to keep soil just moist to the touch. Lower leaves of *D. marginata* will drop if you withhold water too long. Of course, old leaves will drop eventually, anyway, resulting in the angular stem structure that's generally pleasing. As with all houseplants, always use unsoftened, room-temperature water.

Syringe the foliage with water occasionally. In fact, do this with most plants to remove dust that impedes growth. (Don't wash plants with hairy leaves, such as African violets.)

Special helps: Loose, well-drained soil high in organic matter encourages good growth; a general potting soil mixture will suffice. Feed with any complete soluble or liquid houseplant fertilizer every three months, year around.

Start new plants from stem cuttings or by air layering (see pages 88-89 for details). Rejuvenate an overly leggy dracena by cutting it off four to six inches above ground. New growth will sprout on what's left of the old potted stem.

White cottony blobs herald the arrival of mealybugs. Dab them with a cotton swab dipped in rubbing alcohol. If scale insects descend upon your plant, wipe them off with a soft toothbrush dipped in sudsy water, or apply a systemic control.

Corn plant (*Dracaena massangeana*)

Boston fern

Ferns. Among the oldest known plants on earth, ferns were well established before the age of dinosaurs. Rock and coal fossils record their past vastness and grandeur. As the earth's climate changed, ferns—unlike the giant reptiles—adapted to their new surroundings. Many diverse varieties exist, in different sizes, and with widely different forms of foliage in many shades of green.

The most popular fern for home decoration is the Boston (*Nephrolepis exaltata bostoniensis*), which comes in more forms than the other fern classes. Some grow leaves only eight inches long, while other kinds reach four to five feet.

Whitman, curly, and crested ferns are mutations of the Boston fern, which in turn is a mutation of the sword fern. New strains, which are finely divided, curled, and ruffled, have generated new interest in the Boston fern that was most popular at the turn of the century.

Other interesting ferns for indoor use are small brake fern (*Pteris*), which features wiry leaf stems ending in a cluster of green or variegated, elongated leaves. If you want a Victoria brake fern (*Pteris victoriae*), with its jade green fronds striped silvery white, you'll probably find it among plants sold for terrariums. This doesn't mean you must grow it in a terrarium, though, it's beautiful anywhere. You can put it in a small corner on a tabletop where you've been unable to fit anything else.

Maidenhair fern (*Adiantum*) is a small type having wiry leaf stems with long fronds radiating from them in spoke fashion. Small, fan-shaped leaflets line each spoke.

Asplenium, another plant group from which a number of handsome ferns come, includes the bird's-nest fern (*Asplenium nidus*). Its bright green, lance-shaped leaves are whole rather than feathery, and arise stiffly in a whorl from a crown. It prefers more humidity than does the Boston fern; otherwise, it takes the same conditions. In botanical gardens, where ideal environment is maintained, bird's-nest ferns reach four feet. In the home's cooler and drier atmosphere, this fern seldom exceeds 15 inches.

Asplenium myriophyllum, a lacy fern, puts up fronds of 6 to 15 inches and is suitable to grow in a cool greenhouse. The plant does have a tendency to turn brown during winter, though, if humidity is excessive.

Japanese holly-fern (*Cyrtomium falcatum 'Rochefordianum'*) gets its common name from the stiff, varnished look of its 8- to 10-inch fronds. It's easier to grow than the Boston fern and makes less demand for high humidity.

Staghorn fern (*Platycerium vassei*), with its antler-shaped leaves, never fails to attract attention. It grows naturally on trees, so in cultivation attach it to a ball of sphagnum on a board and hang it up. As the plant increases in size, add to the board backing. The staghorn fern forms basal, roundish fronds that turn brown. Don't remove these—they help protect roots and hold moisture in the planting medium.

Light: In nature, ferns grow where light intensity is low. In the

Whitman fern

Bird's-nest fern

Staghorn fern

home, ferns do well under bright light, but not direct sun. In south and west windows, hang a sheer curtain to dilute the intensity of the sun. Boston ferns and others can tolerate a little early morning sun, but it's not necessary. Never expose variegated *Pteris* ferns to sun, just bright light.

Water: Ferns like an even moisture supply to thrive (water less during short, dark winter days). On sunny days, mist foliage early in the morning. Don't mist on dark, damp days, though, or so late in the day that mist remains on leaves overnight. That could invite mold or fungus to form. Once one of these unwelcome guests appears, you might as well destroy the affected plant and start over.

Leaf wilting generally indicates a lack of water. Yellowing, other than that of natural aging or disease, is a sign of excessive moisture or poor drainage. To ensure good drainage for your fern—never allow it to stand in water—use about an inch of clay chips in the bottom of the pot.

To water a staghorn fern, suspend it from a shower head in your bathroom and turn a fine spray of water over the plant, sphagnum, and board. Leave in the shower until dripping stops. Follow this unusual watering procedure twice a week.

Special helps: Feed ferns with care—once every six months with a slow-release should be enough. If you use a liquid houseplant fertilizer, be careful not to use more than stated on container label. And remember: always water your plants *before* applying a fertilizer.

Avoid extremes in temperature and drafty conditions. Keep ferns away from hot air registers. Summer indoor ferns outside only if you can provide them with a filtered light locale sheltered from damaging winds.

Propagate ferns at any time of year by root division. Knock parent plant from its container and remove as much soil as possible. Cut between clumps of fronds or pull apart and pot up the divisions. Some ferns send out long, thin runners that will produce new plants. For these, place a container of moist potting soil next the fern and use long, U-shaped wires to pin the runner to the soil. Keep potting soil moist. When two green leaves develop, cut the runner and pot up.

Ferns dislike heavy soil. Use a commercial mixture high in peat moss, or make your own with two parts peat moss or leaf mold, one part garden loam, and one part perlite or coarse sand. Add a little crushed charcoal to the mixture.

When staghorn fern gets too large, cut out small plants (called "pups") with a sharp knife. Back each pup with a ball of sphagnum, and tie to a board until roots take hold.

Check fronds regularly for fern scale—the small, shell-like coverings of sucking plant mites. Male scales are white; females are brown and pear- or oyster-shaped. If you notice the scales when there are only a few, pick them off or wash off with soapy water, then rinse with clear, tepid water. If your plant is loaded with the pest, destroy it to prevent the problem from spreading throughout your plant collection.

Victoria brake fern

Japanese holly-fern

Asplenium myriophyllum

Celeste fig

Weeping fig (*Ficus benjamina*)

Ficus. Ornamental relatives of the edible fig, the various ficus all become large plants, good for bold accents.

Ficus elastica (rubber plant) and *F. elastica 'decora'* (with broader leaves and red new growth) have long been rated as easy to grow, but really they're not. The assumption has been that the rubber plant would grow in the poorest light and with minimum water. Untrue! A rubber plant needs bright light and regular watering. In its natural environment, it's a big tree, growing in full sun.

F. lyrata (fiddleleaf fig) sports huge, stiff, glossy leaves that demand constant moisture or they turn brown and drop. *F. benjamina* (weeping fig) has small, waxy leaves on pendant branches and is the easiest of this group to manage. Although less fussy about light and water than the others, it will go into a decline if you put it in too dim a light and treat it like a desert plant. Fortunately, *'benjamina'* has recuperative powers and puts out new leaves if you come to the rescue in time. Well-treated plants grow almost continuously.

The Celeste fig boasts bold, handsome leaves that are decorative from spring through fall. They drop just as deciduous trees are losing leaves outside. After they go, however, the angular stems offer their own peculiar beauty throughout dreary winter months. Whether you keep the plant in sight or out of the way when dormant, you'll still have to water it lightly on occasion. To keep this fig happy, add a bit of dolomitic lime once a year to sweeten the potting soil. Celeste's flowers are *inside* the fruit, so don't look for them to foretell fruit formation. Prune only to maintain size and do it during the winter or early spring when the plant is dormant.

Light: All ficus species like bright, indirect sun. Full sun through glass will burn the leaves.

Water: Keep the soil moist to the touch. Frequency of watering depends (as with any houseplant) on the size of the plant and pot and whether the container has drainage and is made of clay, plastic, or ceramic. (See pages 84-85 for watering information relative to these variable factors.)

Special helps: Use a general all-purpose potting soil lightened with a little sand or perlite. Feed three or four times a year with any complete soluble or liquid houseplant food. If your plant grows too fast, space feeding at longer intervals or eliminate altogether. Don't feed Celeste fig during its winter dormancy period.

If your rubber plant or fiddleleaf fig becomes too leggy, air layer it (see instructions on page 89). After removing the rooted top part of the plant, keep watering the original, potted stub—it will sprout new growth.

Take tip cuttings of your weeping fig to start new plants (see page 88). Root them in plain water, vermiculite, or 50-50 vermiculite and peat moss.

For the edible figs, start with nursery-grown root stock.

If mealybugs attack, touch each with a cotton swab dipped in rubbing alcohol. Wash off scale with a wet, sudsy cloth.

Rubber plant (*Ficus elastica*) and Fiddleleaf fig (*Ficus lyrata*); bird's-nest fern (see page 27)

Firefern

Firefern *(Oxalis hedysaroides rubra)*. This shrubby plant is an oxalis, but unlike others in the family, it has red foliage. Little yellow flowers contrast nicely against satiny wine-red leaves.

Light: Firefern needs a sunny window for its foliage to remain a rich red color.

Water: Keep soil evenly moist. Firefern resents soggy soil, so be sure pot has adequate drainage in bottom.

Special helps: Use standard potting mixture. Like most houseplants, the main requirement is a porous medium to allow enough air to get to the roots. Feed sparingly; a light feeding every two or three months should be enough.

Start new plants by taking tip cuttings (see stem cuttings, page 88). Use regular, moist rooting medium and cover with a clear plastic tent until slips are ready to pot up.

Fittonia (nerve plant). This low creeping plant comes handsomely "decorated" with white, pink, or red veins in the leaves. When flowers appear, they grow erect as white spikes.

Light: Grow shade-loving fittonia in a north window or away from sun if near east, south, or west exposures.

Water: Keep the soil moist at all times. Unless your fittonia is growing in the humidity of a terrarium—for which it's admirably suited—set the potted plant on a pebble tray containing wet gravel to help raise the humidity.

Special helps: Feed lightly once or twice a year. Fittonia prefers a porous soil mixture containing plenty of organic matter. Prune to keep under control. Propagate by taking stem cuttings, preferably in the spring. (See page 88.)

Fittonia

Flytrap *(Dionaea muscipula;* Venus flytrap). This small, novelty houseplant can catch and digest flies and other insects, but does not need them to survive. The hinged trap snaps shut when an unsuspecting insect touches the sensitive hairs inside. Digestive juices secreted by the plant finish off the victim, and the trap is set again. Cut off the small flowers that appear in June on tall stems, as they weaken the plant.

Light: Venus flytrap grows in sun in its native Carolinas. Full sun brings out the red coloring inside the leaf traps; if grown mostly in shade, they will be green only.

Water: Never let this plant lack moisture; water every other day. Flytrap prefers high humidity.

Special helps: This is one plant that doesn't need drainage. It grows along the edges of moist sandy bottom land in its natural habitat. In the home, use a wide shallow container without drainage and plant the specimen—not too firmly—in loose, live sphagnum moss. When watering, fill the shallow container with water to wet the moss thoroughly, then pour off excess water. Never fertilize the Venus flytrap.

Propagate by root division. Plants do die naturally as they mature, but new ones will normally take the parent's place. An improper environment—shade, poor potting medium, or air that is too dry—will stunt the flytrap's growth.

Flytrap

Windowful of geraniums

Geraniums *(Pelargonium)*. Many new kinds of this popular pot plant have been developed, the best known of which is the zonal type named for the markings in the foliage. Mainly, leaves are the green, but the colorful zonal sub-group called fancy-leaf geraniums sport variegated foliage. Ivy-leaf varieties, another group of geraniums, perform masterfully in hanging baskets. The scented foliage types give you nutmeg, peppermint, lemon, rose, or other fragrances to enjoy.

Ball-shaped heads of colorful small blooms arise on tall stalks. Zonal kinds come in pink, red, salmon, and white. Ivy-leaved geraniums range from rose-carmine to white.

Light: Geraniums are high-light intensity plants; they thrive in a south or southwest window.

Water: Since they have thick, succulent stems, geraniums can withstand some drought. But for healthy, vigorous growth and blooms, water plants every time soil surface becomes dry. Drainage must be good; they resent waterlogged soil.

Special helps: New geraniums are commonly rooted by taking three-to five-inch growth cuttings from healthy mature plants. Select medium-mature shoots rather than too soft or too old and woody ones. Make a slanting cut just below a leaf to expose more regenerative cells for rooting. Remove lower leaves. Since geraniums are fleshy stemmed, there's no need to rush to place them in a rooting chamber. You can spread them out for a day or two to dry before sticking them in moist rooting medium such as half-and-half perlite-acid peat mix. Dipping the dried cut ends in root-inducing powder first will hasten rooting. Plain water is risky for rooting cuttings, since fleshy stems may rot. Keep rootings out of direct sun.

In six weeks plant the rooted cuttings in 3- or 4-inch pots. Use a potting mixture of three parts garden loam, one part perlite or sand, and one part peat moss or compost. After several days, move into stronger light. When plants are established, cut tips back to induce denser growth. When roots fill pot, shift plants to inch-larger containers.

Geraniums bloom best when slightly pot-bound. Without a daily dose of at least three or four hours of sunshine, your plants will become leggy and refuse to bloom. Pinch back tall stems after blooming to promote branching.

Don't feed your geraniums unless they have stopped growing or the foliage is pale. Even then, use only a small amount of any water-soluble fertilizer (overfeeding will result in leggy plants that produce few blooms). Summer plants outdoors. When you bring them back into the house, isolate for a few weeks to check for plant pests such as whiteflies.

Geranium plants grouped in a decorative pot

How to propagate geraniums

1. *Take 3- to 5-inch tip cuttings*
2. *Insert in rooting medium*
3. *In 6 weeks, pot rooted cuttings*

Gloxinia

Dormancy care. *When your gloxinia stops blooming, withhold water gradually until foliage dries. Store the tuber (in its pot of soil) in a cool (no lower than 50° F.), dark place until new growth starts. Then repot, barely covering crown of tuber, in a 4-inch pot of pre-moistened vermiculite or half-and-half peat and perlite. Set the pot in a warm, softly lighted spot; water only enough to keep the vermiculite moist. Encasing each pot in a plastic sack until the tuber is rooted will often aid plant growth. Don't let soil waterlog, or the tuber may rot.*

Gloxinia (*Sinningia*). One of the most spectacular of all houseplants, this relative of the African violet blooms freely, producing flowers in a multitude of hues—red, purple, blue, red with white edging, and other bicolors. Velvety leaves arise from tubers.

Light: Plants need bright light, but no direct sunlight. Too little light creates leggy stems you'll need to stake.

Water: Gloxinias like evenly moist soil, but they can't stand being waterlogged. Avoid getting water on the hairy foliage or atop the tuber, as it may rot—a common gloxinia problem.

Special helps: Use the same commercial potting soil mixture designed for African violets. Soil high in humus is best.

Apply liquid houseplant fertilizer as soon as you see small flower buds developing. Feed lightly every few weeks.

Being tropical plants, gloxinias prefer plenty of humidity and warmth of at least 70° F. during the day.

You can root new plants by taking leaf cuttings from a mature plant after it blooms. A tuber develops at the base of a leaf cutting if started either in water or a soil mixture. Plant rooted leaf in a 3-inch pot with new tuber slightly below soil level. Brace parent leaf with sticks; remove it after new foliage appears.

Hibiscus.

Hibiscus. This shrubby hollyhock relative produces showy four-to eight-inch blooms in such colors as red, orange, violet, apricot, and pink. Flowering primarily takes place in summer and fall on young shoots. Even when the plant is not in bloom, though, the dark green glossy leaves, which tend to be oval, pointed, and toothed along the edge, make the plant attractive. Chinese hibiscus (*Hibiscus rosa-sinensis*), one of the best-known varieties, attains a height of about four feet as a potted plant indoors. Single and double-flowered varieties are available, too.

Light: Sun is essential for hibiscus to bloom. But if you don't have a sunny window, the hibiscus is also a lovely foliage plant.

Water: Keep soil on the dry side during winter months of resting, and keep the plant in a cool spot. In early March, cut plant back one-half, repot in fresh potting mixture, and water. Syringe top daily to speed new growth. Keep soil evenly moist during warm months by watering freely.

Special helps: Chinese hibiscus likes warm sun during its spring and summer growth period. During winter, keep it in a cool room where temperature doesn't go below 50° F.

Use a standard soil mixture for potting. Feed moderately at three-week intervals during bud and bloom period.

To propagate, take three-inch stem cuttings; remove lower leaves and stick in moist rooting medium of half perlite and half peat. Cover with clear plastic tent for high humidity.

When rooted, use three-inch pots for planting. When young shoots reach six inches tall, pinch out terminal and side tips to make plant bushy. Mist tops each morning to encourage development of new growth. After blooming, prune back to keep plant compact and to promote new foliage and more flowers. When plant gets too big, prune it back to the size you want.

Chinese hibiscus

Hoya

Hoya (*Hoya carnosa*; wax-plant). Among the dozen or so varieties of hoyas, leaves range from thick and waxy to long and narrow to almost round, and the colors from shades of green to variegated green and white. The waxy, star-shaped blooms form into rounded, white clusters in spring and early summer.

Light: Place your hoya near a window that receives strong, indirect light.

Water: Let the plant dry out slightly between waterings. To encourage spring blooming, keep the soil fairly dry in late fall and early winter.

Special helps: Hoyas respond well to training on a trellis. Start new plants readily from stem cuttings at any time of year. Cut 8- to 10-inch sections of stem just below a pair or group of leaves. Set these in a rooting medium that is kept constantly moist. In five or six weeks, they should be rooted well enough to plant in loose potting soil.

For a faster start, you can bury the base of a leaf cluster in a pot of soil set beside the parent plant and postpone cutting the stem until new roots form. With any young hoya, expect to wait a year or two for first blooms.

Hoya

Ivy and ivy-like vines. These trailing plants extend your garden far above floor-standing specimens. Train some climbers on supports, too. English ivy (*Hedera helix*), a true ivy, shows many variations of leaf shapes and sizes. You can grow variegated as well as green foliages that either branch freely or stay compact.

German ivy (*Senecio*) has thin, bright green leaves shaped like those of English ivy. Swedish ivy (*Plectranthus australis*) and Creeping charlie (*Pilea nummulariaefolia*) are very similar, with their roundish, scallop-edged, green leaves.

Devil's ivy (*Scindapsus*; golden pothos) often is mistaken for philodendron. Leaves tend to be heart-shaped, but with generally brighter green leaves, variegated with yellow. One kind, 'Marble Queen', is whitish, flecked with green.

Grape ivy (*Cissus*) has three green, sharp-toothed leaflets, also tendrils. Rust-colored veins show underneath leaves.

Wandering Jew *(Tradescantia, Zebrina)* sparks up a grouping of all-green foliage with its coloration ranging from purple, white, red, brown and gold, blue-green, to silver.

Light: English ivies do well in filtered light; a north window is fine. A little cool, east sun exposure won't hurt them. Grape ivy, Devil's ivy, and German ivy like similar low-light conditions. Swedish ivy prefers bright, indirect sunlight. Wandering Jew will grow well in shade, but bright light and east sun will intensify coloration in the foliage.

Water: Keep ivies evenly moist. Water as soon as soil surface feels dry. Be sure surplus water drains away freely.

Special helps: Start new vines by taking six- to eight-inch cuttings. Select medium-mature growth, remove a couple of the lower leaves, and insert in a regular rooting medium such as a mixture of half perlite and half peat. Water and cover with a clear plastic tent; keep in a moderately warm place out of direct sun. When cuttings are rooted, plant in small pots, using a general all-purpose potting soil mixture.

If you have trouble rooting English ivy, fill a drinking glass with water, crimp aluminum foil over the top, punch a small hole in the foil, and insert cutting into the water. Pot up as soon as roots form.

Avoid feeding ivies during the short days of winter. As the days become longer, the plant will be able to use small amounts of nutrients. Start with first feeding in February and give moderate feedings every one or two months.

During winter, English and German ivies prefer cooler temperatures—45 to 50° F. Misting both sides of foliage daily helps increase humidity and also helps discourage red spider mites, which are a common problem, especially on English ivies. The pest multiplies rapidly when the plant is in warm, dry air. An infested plant deteriorates and close inspection reveals tiny webs. Test for presence of the bug by holding a white sheet of paper underneath leaves and tapping vines sharply. Look closely for tiny specks crawling on the paper. To control, bathe the plant weekly in soapy water or use a systemic insecticide.

English Ivy (*Hedera helix*)

Devil's Ivy (*Scindapsus*)

Creeping charlie (*Pilea nummulariaefolia*) and Wandering Jew (*Tradescantia*)

Jade plant and three Kalanchoes Irwin Hybrid 'Rachel'

Jade plant (*Crassula argentea*). This succulent, with jade-colored, fleshy leaves, often resembles a small tree as it branches gracefully to a height of three feet or more. Outside in warm areas, this crassula can grow to six feet or more. Mature plants may produce tiny pink flowers in fall if you summer plants outdoors (ease them into the sun gradually).

Light: Jade plant performs best with some direct sunlight.

Water: As with all succulents, the danger is overwatering. Let soil almost dry between thorough waterings. Once a week or once every other week should be adequate.

Special helps: Plants will usually live for years, even when rootbound. Repot at any season. Any all-purpose potting mixture will accommodate the jade plant—it isn't particular. Don't feed, except lightly in summer, as the plant can grow excessively if encouraged too much. Be guided by the rate of growth and the size of plant you can manage inside. Air layer to start new plants, or take tip cuttings and root them in a perlite-soil mixture. See pages 88-89 for instructions.

Kalanchoe (*Kalanchoe blossfeldiana*). This succulent features thick, waxy leaves with smooth or scalloped reddish edges. Clusters of small cherry-, orange-red-, yellow-, or apricot-colored florets last a long time. Like the poinsettia, kalanchoe will bloom only when subjected to the shortest days of the year. They normally bloom in spring. To coax them into December bloom, shorten the long days of mid-August to October by covering the pots with black cloth from 5 p.m. to 7 a.m. daily. The plant will not bloom if it gets any light at night —even one minute of light during the night can affect it.

Light: Give kalanchoe full sun in spring, fall, and winter, but avoid direct sun during the hottest part of summer.

Water: Keep watering until the blooms fade and let soil dry between waterings. Then, keep plant on the dry side for two months if you want to carry it over another year. Water just enough to keep the leaves from shriveling.

Special helps: Use a standard potting mixture; soil should be loose. Feed occasionally from spring into fall months. Give more when plant blooms. Kalanchoe prefers cool temperatures —about 50° F. at night and around 70° F. during the day.

Propagate by seed or by leaf or stem cuttings. For best plants, start from seed, sowing in sterile media such as vermiculite in January for blooms the following winter. As soon as a couple of true leaves form, lift seedling carefully from the rooting medium and plant in 2½-inch pot. Move into successively ½-inch-larger pots as roots start to crowd walls of pot. Finish in about 4-inch pots.

Plants that are held over for another year after blooming won't be attractive. To get better-looking new plants, take leaf or stem cuttings, then discard the parent plant. Root the cuttings in a sterile perlite-soil mixture. Place the cuttings out of direct sun and keep medium moist. Pot up the cuttings when rooted.

Eliminate drainage stains. Take steps to prevent water damage caused by spillovers and seepage from your freshly watered plants. One way to avoid trouble is to set clay pots inside waterproof jardinieres or baskets fitted with varnished saucers. Place large, heavy plants such as six-foot palms or philodendrons on platforms or trays equipped with casters. The air space below the platform keeps water from collecting under the plant; casters let you move it easily.

Maranta

Give plants breathing room.
When you're grouping your houseplant collection, be sure to give each plant the space it needs. Don't jam specimens together with two neighbors touching leaves. Instead, space plants out so all the growing tips have room to develop and unfold normally.

Distorted new growth may result if you force growing tips to stretch around a nearby obstacle in order to unfold.

Mimosa

Maranta (*Maranta leuconeura kerchoveana;* prayer plant). Maranta's exotic leaves, which fold up at night as if praying, give it its nickname. Foliage comes with various colored patterns—light green leaves with dark brush-like markings on both sides of the main vein, pronounced light-colored veins against dark-colored leaves, and even a red-veined one.

Light: Avoid direct sun. A bit of cool morning sun won't hurt, but maranta doesn't need bright light.

Water: A moist, humid atmosphere is best. Mist daily. Use tepid water when either watering or misting. Keep soil on the dry side during short winter days; otherwise, keep moist.

Special helps: Start new plants by root division (see page 88) in late winter before new growth begins. Use a peaty mixture such as one containing one part loam soil, two parts peat moss, and one part perlite or coarse sand. Prune off straggly leaves.

Give a light application of houseplant fertilizer only during long summer days and not more than once a month.

Mimosa (*Mimosa pudica;* sensitive plant; shame plant). Mimosa is usually classified as a plant for children, but everyone finds it entertaining to watch the leaflets close up when touched with a pencil or finger. Although short-lived, the plant grows from seed so easily that you can always have a supply on hand. Flowers resemble little purplish puffs.

Light: Mimosa prefers a shady rather than a sunny climate, and grows well in indirect light.

Water: Correct watering provides the real secret to success with mimosa. Keep it evenly moist at all times; don't overwater or underwater or you'll soon lose your plant.

Special helps: Purchase seeds from garden centers and nurseries. When planting, put four or five seeds in a four-inch pot filled with all-purpose potting soil. Seeds will germinate in seven days, and plants will produce their lavender-pink fuzzy flowers in about six months. If all seeds germinate, transfer two or three into each three-inch pot, as one plant looks skimpy.

Monkey-puzzle (*Araucaria araucana*).

Legend has it that even a monkey would be puzzled as to how to climb this intricately branched tree that adapts well to container gardening. Unlike its uniform cousin, the Norfolk pine, the monkey-puzzle reaches out irregularly, and the glossy, pointed leaves grow in all directions. The leaves are sharp enough to discourage the casual handling that many houseplants resent.

Light: Ideally, put it in a spot away from direct sun. This plant thrives in almost any setting, though. It's not forever bending toward the light source, so you don't have to turn it often to correct its growth pattern. If a sunny window is the only location available, that will do—just water the plant more often than you normally would.

Water: Water thoroughly once a week—more if in the sun.

Special helps: Monkey-puzzle isn't fussy—use an all-purpose potting soil. Its growth is slow, so don't worry about introducing this "tree" to your indoor plant collection.

Monkey-puzzle

Norfolk Island pine (*Araucaria excelsa* or *A. heterophylla*).

Limbs project from the trunk of this slow-growing evergreen tree in tiers like spokes on a wheel.

Light: Avoid direct sunlight indoors or outdoors.

Water: This tree tolerates generous watering as long as surplus drains away readily. Water less during winter.

Special helps: Norfolk Island pine is one of the easiest plants to grow indoors. It's fairly trouble-free as long as its desired environmental conditions are met. If needles on lower limbs all start to turn brown, cut off those branches flush with the trunk. Also make sure the plant isn't potbound, that drainage is good, and that the soil hasn't been kept too dry.

If your plant becomes straggly, cut 12 to 15 inches off the top and root the cutting in a half-and-half mixture of peat and perlite. Discard the parent plant. Shift the rooted cutting progressively to inch-larger pots every year until an 8-inch pot is used. Use standard potting mixture. You can root branches, but you will get a one-sided curved shape rather than an upright, symmetrical form.

You also can grow these plants from seeds, but the resulting tree may not assume the dwarf, compact habit of the parent.

Feed your Norfolk Island pine no more than once a month and only during active growth periods of spring and summer.

Norfolk Island Pine

Cattleya orchid

Cymbidium orchids

Orchids.

Orchids. It's high time the myth about orchids was dispelled. True, they are glamorous, but there's no need to equate glamor with being hard to grow. Some are as easy to grow indoors as other houseplants: the moth orchid (phalaenopsis—in white, pink, and yellow); lady-slipper (paphiopedilum or cypripedium—yellow, green, mahogany, solid, and speckled); and miniature cymbidium (white, yellow, tones of red, and green). After growing these, go on to the florists' orchid (cattleya), which is more of a challenge. Avoid the regular, big cymbidiums; they need a chilling in August-September that's hard to provide in many parts of the country.

Light: Different types of orchids require different amounts of light. Moth orchid likes bright, but no direct sunlight. Lady-slipper prefers indirect light. Miniature cymbidium wants very bright light. Cattleya insists on light bright enough that foliage becomes yellow-green (lush green signals insufficient light, and, as a result, no flowers).

Water: Keep the potting medium moist. Since it is porous, water runs right through. So water every other day—possibly every day in hot weather. Apply room temperature water at the sink and let excess drain out. Do not let water stand in leaf axils of moth orchid and lady-slipper, or they'll rot. Cymbidiums and cattleyas have bulbs (true term is pseudobulbs); water runs off them easily.

Special helps: Most orchids don't grow in soil. They're potted in fir bark or tree-fern chunks (sometimes osmunda). Purchase potting media from any mail-order orchid firm or from any nursery selling orchids. When you buy an orchid plant, be sure it's already potted, not bare root (unless you've already had experience potting them up). The medium the potted plant comes in will last at least two years before breaking down and needing replacement.

Use special orchid fertilizer, available wherever orchids are sold. Follow instructions on the package. Orchids are heavy feeders, but the time and money spent feeding them will result in more robust plants and longer blooming periods.

Humidity is a must for orchids. Provide it by setting the plants on pebbles in a tray of water. Keep the water level below the top of the pebbles, as the roots of most orchid varieties will rot if kept constantly moist. Mist foliage regularly, in the morning, so plants can dry off during the day. (Mold or fungus could form if foliage remains wet overnight continually.) Orchids like air circulation; but keep them away from drafts.

If scale insects attack (hard-bodied brown specks on the leaves), rub them off with a soft old towel dipped in sudsy water.

Orchids propagate by division. Lady-slipper makes offsets; divide only when pot is crowded. Moth orchids produce offsets and sometimes sprout plantlets on old stems (remove when roots develop to about a half inch, and pot up individually). Cattleya and cymbidium bloom on successive pseudobulbs (old ones die after flowering); divide rhizome into sections, with each portion having at least three or four bulbs.

Phalaenopsis, "moth orchid" (top) and cypripedium, "lady-slipper"

Fishtail palm (foreground) and areca (back corner)

Palms.

Palms. A glamorous aura surrounds these dramatic plants. Not only do they create a lush tropical atmosphere, but they're easy to grow if you follow the culture tips below. The varieties shown on these pages are all suited to container growing, indoors or out. And decorative palms develop slowly, so you can enjoy them for years to come.

The fishtail palm in the foreground on the opposite page is unique, with jagged-edged leaflets that suggest exotic goldfish. The areca in the background corner has multiple trunks with dense leaves. Allow space for this one; it will in time bush out to make a veritable jungle all on its own.

The European fan palm, top right, has a number of things going for it: its bluish color, its extremely slow growth, its tolerance of sun (if exposed gradually), its drought resistance, and its minimum maintenance requirements. Potentially a 15-footer, this palm stays at three to five feet in a container. Its stark, rugged look can lend force and a sculptural accent to a sparsely furnished setting.

The lady palm, center right, is a tough old aristocrat. She likes dappled light best. Canes multiply slowly on this split-leaved fan palm. The plant in time reaches eight feet tall, but growth is so slow that it's nothing to worry about. Like all other palms, she welcomes a summer vacation outdoors if sheltered from full sun and potentially damaging winds.

The parlor palm is ornamental even in the seedling stage—when most other palms look like broadleaved weeds. It grows slowly to three or four feet and is ideal for only moderate light. It can go outdoors to a shady corner in summer.

The umbrella palm (see page 48), so-called because of the marked downward curve of its leaves, is one of the numerous feather palms. It does well indoors with good bright light, but no direct sun. It can vacation outdoors after the temperature stays above 50° F. day and night. To prevent burning, it needs filtered shade, such as from overhead lathing.

The howea (usually, but wrongly, called kentia) remains an old reliable for indoor decoration (see page 49). It profits—as does any palm—by being sunk in the soil outdoors during summer months. Plant it rim deep in a shady place in company with other filtered-light lovers such as crotons and fibrous begonias.

Notched stalks explain the common name of the bamboo palms (see photo on page 49). They're among the most durable and adaptable palms. They take well to low-level light conditions and survive on less water than other palms.

Light: Indoors, provide bright light (even a bit of full sun in winter) year-round. Shelter with filtered shade outdoors in summer, particularly the parlor and bamboo types. The European fan palm takes full sun if offered gradually.

Water: Moisture is of prime importance. Palms are *not* desert plants, so provide plenty of water and you'll avoid leaf browning (other than natural dying from age). A plant in a 9-inch pot requires a quart and a half of water once a week. If you can get

European fan palm

Lady palm

Parlor palm

Umbrella palm

Howea palm (see page 22 for adjacent crotons)

the pot to the sink, pour in another quart and let it run out the bottom hole to leach unwanted chemicals from the soil. But don't let the potting medium remain soggy over long periods of time.

Special helps: A slow-release food for houseplants applied according to manufacturer's directions every three or four months year-round, will keep your palms healthy. You'll find that indoor palms make new growth in winter. Growth is slow, varying from one species to another. When your plants near the maximum size you want, feed them just once a year in spring. Go easier on feeding the potential giants (fishtail and fan palms) than the naturally short ones (parlor and bamboo). Exercise restraint, too, with the wide-spreaders (howea and areca).

Soil must be porous; mix in sand or perlite, if needed. Otherwise, lots of water can mean soggy soil, and that means death for a palm.

Browning of leaves is usually the result of insufficient watering. Chemicals in the water may also cause trouble. Control this by leaching as described above in the section on water. Too-dry air can also be responsible. Mist the foliage daily. If only small tips of fronds turn brown, snip off brown areas with scissors. Don't bother trying to propagate palms.

Bamboo palm

Pandanus. Also called screw pine, the arching leaves of the pandanus form a perfect spiral off the plant's crown, creating a beautiful fountain effect that will spread 30 inches. Variegated variety, *Pandanus veitchi,* sports white markings.

Light: Give pandanus bright, indirect sunlight.

Water: Let soil almost dry between waterings. Mist daily.

Special helps: When your table-size pandanus outgrows its location, graduate it to a pedestal or jardiniere and use it as a floor specimen. Start new plants from offsets that form around the base of the parent. Unpot the mature plant, and remove the offsets with a sharp knife. These offspring send down aerial roots that grow in the soil, so be sure to get as many of these roots as possible by gently loosening the soil ball as you pull the offsets free. A single plant will often put out five or six offsets at one time. Pot up the plantlets individually, using an all-purpose potting mixture.

Pandanus

Passion flower (*Passiflora*). Early missionaries imagined the Passion of Christ in the structure of this spectacular flower. The petals symbolized the 10 apostles at the crucifixion, the rays of the corona the crown of thorns, the five anthers the wounds, the three stigmas the nails, the coiling tendrils the cords and whips, and the five-lobed leaves the cruel hands of the persecutors. Each flower lasts only a day, unless you pick it before it folds up at night and refrigerate its base in a shallow dish of water. The vine blooms from summer into late fall. Provide a trellis or other support for the plant to climb. Prune back when vine becomes inconveniently large. You'll then have to wait for flowers, which appear only on the new growth.

Light: Passion flower thrives in full sun.

Water: Water when soil starts to dry out.

Special helps: Feed every two months from March to September. Withhold food if vine grows too fast. Root 6-inch stem cuttings from midsummer into fall. Plant in a general potting soil mixture. Summer your passion flower outdoors if you wish. If mealybugs build their white cottony homes on the plant, kill by touching each with an alcohol-saturated cotton swab.

Pedilanthus

Pedilanthus. Nicknamed Devil's backbone, the zigzag stems of this slow-growing plant may reach 2 to 3 feet. The white variegation of the pointed, oval, green leaves turns pink in strong light. Pedilanthus may drop its leaves in fall, leaving sculptural bare stems. New leaves appear in 4 to 6 weeks. Pedilanthus never becomes bushy; use it as a vertical accent.

Light: Supply bright light for best leaf color. If kept in low-light areas, the foliage will turn solid green.

Water: Keep just moist to prevent premature leaf drop.

Special helps: Feed with any complete soluble or liquid houseplant food in early spring and midsummer. Propagate pedilanthus by rooting 3- to 5-inch stem cuttings anytime. Pot up the rooted starts in an all-purpose houseplant potting soil, or grow the cut stems in charcoal-sweetened water.

Passion flower

Pellionia. Grow this creeper for its showy foliage which is colored dark bronze or purplish or is green with silvery-green centers. Pellionia is less aggressive than its relative, baby's tears. Use it singly on a low table, in a hanging basket, or as a groundcover around a large potted palm, dracena, or ficus.

Light: Pellionia prefers filtered light or shade.

Water: Keep soil slightly moist at all times or leaves will drop. Avoid soggy soil to prevent stem rot.

Special helps: Feed with any complete soluble or liquid houseplant fertilizer once a month from March to September. Take stem cuttings anytime (see page 88). Pot up the rooted starts in rich, sandy, well-drained potting soil.

Peperomias. Varied foliage makes this plant family one of the most popular with indoor gardeners. Both upright and trailing types are available. Tall, skinny, stalk-like blooms add a touch of novelty to the stemless peperomias. Thickish, succulent leaves may be smooth, glossy green, variegated, corrugated, or deeply ridged, with green, pink, or red stems. Shown in the photo, clockwise from the left: *Peperomia obtusifolia, P. griseo-argentea, P. caperata, P. obtusifolia variegata,* and *P. sandersi*—the popular "watermelon peperomia." Dozens of other varieties also are available.

Most intriguing are the wrinkle-leaved peperomias, such as Emerald Ripple (*P. caperata*). Little Fantasy is a shorter variety; Tri-color features variegated leaves on red leaf stems.

Watermelon peperomia (*P. sandersi*) reaches 8 to 10 inches tall, with leaves striped like green-and-white watermelons.

Ivy peperomia (*P. griseo-argentea*) resembles the wrinkle-leaved type, but grows taller, and the larger leaves are less deeply wrinkled.

The waxy-leaved peperomias, such as *P. obtusifolia,* become almost a foot tall and tend to trail when mature.

Light: Supply medium to bright light, but no direct sun. A bright north window is fine, but diffuse intense sun elsewhere.

Water: Succulent peperomias rot easily if kept too wet. Allow the soil to dry a little during the short days of winter when the plant is dormant. When new growth starts in February, keep the soil evenly moist and be sure drainage is good. Peperomias like humidity and so make desirable terrarium plants.

Special helps: Feed no more than once a month during periods of growth with any complete soluble or liquid houseplant fertilizer. Don't feed during winter dormancy.

Stem rot may occur at the soil line or below. If the problem is advanced before you notice it, take cuttings and discard the plant. Stunted plants with leaves disfigured with concentric zonal markings are victims of ring spot, a virus disease. Destroy the infected plant; do not take cuttings.

Propagate stemless peperomias by dividing the crowns of mature plants in early spring or by rooting leaf cuttings. Pick a medium-size leaf and leave a length of "stem" attached. Stick the cutting in moist rooting medium such as sand or vermiculite,

Pellionia

Persian shield

Peperomias

with the base of the leaf just above the surface. Cover with a clear plastic bag held away from the foliage by several stakes. This helps maintain humidity. Keep the medium moist. Put in a warm, bright place, out of direct sun. When rooted, pot up, using standard soil mixture. Root 3-inch tip cuttings on peperomias with main stems.

Persian shield (*Strobilanthes dyerianus*). Showy, but not gaudy, the iridescent green, blue, and amethyst foliage of Persian shield gives a lift to a collection of plain green plants. The violet flowers, which appear infrequently, or not at all, take a back seat to the colorful leaves.

Light: Give Persian shield bright, but not direct sunlight.

Water: Water when soil starts to dry out. Leaf edges will turn brown if your Persian shield stays thirsty too long.

Special helps: Feed this plant once in late spring or midsummer with any complete soluble or liquid houseplant fertilizer. Overfeeding encourages rapid growth, which results in unattractively leggy plants with smaller leaves.

Root stem cuttings to start new plants. Pot up in all-purpose houseplant potting soil. If mealybugs infest your Persian shield, touch each with an alcohol-saturated cotton swab.

Philodendrons and a monstera

Philodendrons. Natives of the rain forests, the popular philodendrons adapt well to the less humid environment of homes and apartments. Foliage comes in a variety of sizes, shapes, and range of greens. Leaves may be whole or lobed.

The over 200 varieties of philodendrons fall into one of two categories: trailing or self-heading. *Philodendron oxycardium,* the most common vine or trailing form grown in homes, features smooth, heart-shaped leaves. A self-heading or self-supporting philodendron, such as *P. selloum*—commonly called saddle-leaved philodendron—sends up large leaves on tall stems arising from a center rosette.

The photo at left shows half a dozen philodendrons, plus a *Monstera deliciosa,* often called split-leaf philodendron or Swiss cheese plant, center left. Monstera's not really a philodendron, but its cultural requirements are similar.

In front of the monstera sits a fiddle leaf philodendron *(P. panduraeforme),* beside a velvet leaf philodendron *(P. micans).* Wendland *(P. wendlandi)* occupies the center, next to 'Florida' *(P. 'Florida compacta').* The long, slightly twisted stems of imbe *(P. imbe)* jut out from the back right, neighbor to a 'Red Emerald' *(P. hastatum)* on a totem pole.

Light: While philodendrons will tolerate shade, they do best in bright, indirect light. Avoid hot, direct sun.

Water: Philodendrons need moist, well-drained soil. If drainage is good enough that surplus water drains away readily, water two or three times a week. Large philodendrons and monstera benefit from a support wrapped with moist sphagnum moss. When you water the soil, water the sphagnum, too. It provides extra humidity, and roots tend to grow into it. Misting leaves regularly with water helps raise the humidity around the plant. The common, small-leaved, trailing philodendron will grow in the humid air of a terrarium for years.

Special helps: Philodendrons like an acid, peat-based soil, so add some crushed charcoal to a standard all-purpose potting mixture. And for best results, feed these plants every three or four months with a houseplant fertilizer.

Many self-heading types, such as the selloum, produce offsets around the base of the parent plant. Either transplant these offsets or, propagate by air layering the thick stems. For the trailing varieties, root stem cuttings to obtain additional plants. (See page 88 for instructions.)

Low humidity or waterlogged soil may cause leaves to dry up and turn brown. To remedy this, trim with scissors. If new growth has smaller leaves, give plant brighter light.

White cottony tufts indicate mealybugs. Destroy these pests by touching each with a cotton swab dipped in rubbing alcohol. Use soapy water to wash scale insects off.

Keep foliage free of dust by occasionally wiping leaves off with a soft, wet cloth.

Some large varieties, such as selloum and monstera, send out long, rope-like aerial roots above ground. Stick these into the soil, or clip them off if you don't like their looks.

Vining philodendron

Pleomele

Pickaback plant

Pickaback plant (*Tolmiea menziesi;* piggyback plant; mother-of-thousands). Plantlets develop atop the base of each mature, long-stemmed, hairy leaf. In time, smaller plantlets appear on top of the earlier ones; hence, the common names of this compact foliage plant. Inconspicuous flowers may appear.

Light: Give your pickaback bright, indirect light.

Water: The numerous thin leaves wilt easily unless you maintain an evenly moist soil. If the plant does wilt, water thoroughly and it should revive.

Special helps: Apply a regular houseplant fertilizer about once a month. Follow label directions carefully.

Propagate pickaback by pegging the plantlets on runners into moist potting soil in adjacent containers. After the plantlets have rooted, sever the runners. Or, take leaf cuttings. To do this, remove a mature leaf along with several inches of leaf stem. Then, stick the stem into a moist, sterile rooting medium such as vermiculite, with the leaf blade touching the surface. After roots form, pot up plant in a standard houseplant soil mixture.

Pleomele ('Song of India'). This tough foliage plant resembles a dracena, but with shorter leaves. Leaves emanate along the length of the willowy stems, and dense clusters of leathery green leaves protrude from the stem ends (one variety features variegated leaves). Pleomele grows slowly. Give the stems support when they start to bend over. Given proper support, pleomele will grow in water as well as soil.

Light: While pleomele will tolerate low light intensity for years, a healthier-looking plant will result in medium to bright light, including some east sun.

Water: Keep the soil slightly moist—avoid sogginess. Pleomele reacts best to high humidity.

Special helps: This plant needs little feeding. A standard houseplant fertilizer used once every two months only in spring and summer should be adequate.

Root a new plant in spring by cutting off a four-inch stem tip. Strip off the lower leaves and insert the stem in a moist, sterile rooting medium such as vermiculite until rooted. Or, place the cutting in water and pot up as soon as short roots form. Use a regular houseplant potting soil mixture.

Podocarpus

Podocarpus

Podocarpus (*Podocarpus macrophyllus maki;* Chinese podocarpus). Use the versatile podocarpus in a dish garden when the plant is small. Grow the mature specimen in a large pot; it shouldn't need repotting for years. Left alone, it will eventually reach five or six feet tall. To obtain shorter, denser growth, prune in early spring before new growth starts. The bright green, juvenile leaves turn dark as the plant matures.

Light: Podocarpus thrives with four or more hours of direct sunlight daily, but it will tolerate indirect or bright artificial light in the home.

Water: Keep the soil barely wet, and check the plant daily to be sure it has an even supply of moisture.

Special helps: Repot a rootbound podocarpus in early spring, before new growth starts. Use a standard all-purpose potting mixture. Start new plants from stem cuttings in the fall; see page 88 for propagation instructions.

Pony tail

Pony tail

Pony tail (*Beaucarnea recurvata;* elephant-foot tree). Want an easy-care houseplant? Then try the hardy, palmlike pony tail. In time it will reach your ceiling, but it grows so slowly you'll have a long time to enjoy it before that happens.

As the trunk gradually elongates, the bulbous base swells in an irregular manner. This attention-catching shape prompts questions, so be prepared to answer any queries. As the plant matures, the fountain of leaves becomes steadily more dense.

Light: Give your pony tail bright light, or even direct sun for a few hours daily.

Water: Pony tail can endure your forgetfulness, since the swelling, bulbous base serves as a water reservoir. Add water only when the soil feels dry.

Special helps: Pony tail likes a container seemingly too small for its size. When it does appear rootbound, repot in the spring before new growth begins. Use a standard houseplant potting mixture. Feed once a year in the spring.

Portulacaria

Portulacaria. This succulent shrub resembles an old favorite, the jade plant, but has smaller leaves and more angular growth. The upright branches and shrubby appearance give this minimum-care plant considerable sculptural interest.

Light: In its native South African climate, portulacaria does best in well-drained soil in hot, dry areas. Indoors, provide the brightest light possible short of direct sun.

Water: Too much water will cause root rot and eventual death, so water only when the soil dries out completely.

Special helps: Take four- or five-inch tip cuttings to propagate this low-humidity, little-care plant (see page 88 for rooting details). When rooted, pot up the starts in a porous potting mix of ⅓ sand and ⅔ soil. Add a shard or gravel to the bottom of the pot for drainage.

Purple passion *(Gynura; velvet plant).* This colorful foliage plant exists both as a vine *(Gynura sarmentosa)* and as a small shrub *(G. aurantiaca).* Bright purple hairs cover the elongated, scalloped leaves. Both types bear small orange flowers infrequently, and make good candidates for hanging pots.

Light: To maintain the bright purple color, place the plant where it receives three or four hours of direct sun daily. If you wish, summer your purple passion outdoors where it receives some east sun.

Water: Keep soil barely moist at all times—never soggy.

Special helps: Feed your purple passion lightly no more than once a month. Apply water to the soil before fertilizing, as with any other plant you're feeding.

For more dense plants, prune the stem ends. To obtain more plants, root the cuttings any time of year. (See page 88 for details.) When roots reach about an inch, pot up, using a standard potting soil mixture.

Kill mealybugs in their white cottony nests by touching each bug with a cotton swab dipped in rubbing alcohol.

Purple passion

Sanchezia *(Sanchezia nobilis).* This multistemmed shrub will reach three to five feet tall and almost as wide. Creamy yellow veins grace the long green leaves attached to red stems. Red bracts trim the yellow flowers.

Light: Provide filtered or semishady light.

Water: This woody plant demands high amounts of moisture, so water when the soil surface starts to dry out.

Special helps: Feed with any complete soluble or liquid houseplant fertilizer twice a year—in late spring and midsummer. Take tip cuttings in summer to start new plants (see page 88). When rooted, pot up, using a standard houseplant potting mix. Mature plants tend to become leggy as their lower leaves drop off. When this happens, place a lower plant in front of the sanchezia to hide the bare stems.

If red spider mites attack, retaliate by carrying the plant outside and hosing the pests away. Wipe off scale insects with a

Sanchezia behind a waffle plant (page 69)

Sansevieria

soft cloth dipped in sudsy water. Kill mealybugs by touching each with an alcohol-saturated cotton swab.

Sansevieria (snake plant, hemp plant, mother-in-law tongue). Call it whatever you want, sansevieria endures when other plants falter. Relegate it to dim daylight, haphazard watering, heat, dust, dry air—it survives. About the only way to kill it is by drowning it with too much water.

Pamper it with bright light—even up to an hour of direct sun daily—water thoroughly about every two weeks, clean its leaves regularly, and sansevieria will reward your attentiveness with lush, vigorous growth. A potbound, mature plant will even send up tall spikes of dainty, white, fragrant blooms.

Light: This tough plant will exist for a long time in dim corners, but give it bright light, even east sun, if possible.

Water: Since sansevierias are succulent, they like low humidity. Keep the soil on the dry side. Water only once every two weeks during the dormancy period of fall and winter. When new growth appears in spring, increase the amount of water. As with all plants, apply unsoftened, room-temperature water. Cold water shocks the plant's system; softened water contains harmful chemicals that may be stockpiled in soil each time you water.

Special helps: Feed no more than once a month during the spring and summer active growth periods.

Divide roots of a mature plant to increase your supply.

Well-hung plants. A potful of wet soil weighs more than you'd imagine. Prevent hanging plant fall-out by screwing hooks directly into solid wood wall studs or ceiling joists when possible. Otherwise, use screw anchors or toggle bolts—found in any hardware department.

Avoid dripping seepage when you water by hanging only waterproof containers or pots equipped with saucers to catch the excess moisture.

Spathiphyllum

Strawberry saxifrage

Snowflake plant (*Trevesia sanderi*). This slow-growing, small tree, with one of the most intricate leaf patterns in the whole plant kingdom, never fails to intrigue. Place it out of the line of traffic, though, as thorns are murderous.

Light: Provide diffused light. Direct sun burns foliage.

Water: Let the soil start to dry out between waterings. Once every week to 10 days is adequate for a large plant.

Special helps: Feed once a month from March to September. Propagation is rather difficult. Try air layering (see page 89 for instructions). Pot up in a standard all-purpose potting soil mixture. Be wary of the thorns when working with your snowflake plant.

If mealybugs erect their white, cottony edifices, destroy by touching each pest with a cotton swab dipped in rubbing alcohol. Use a soft towel dipped in sudsy water to wipe off any scale insects that appear.

Spathiphyllum (*Spathiphyllum patini; S. 'Clevelandi'*). Like the more common calla lily, white petal-like leaves envelope the true flowers which are the central yellow columns. The variety Mauna Loa blooms intermittently all year.

Light: Provide bright light in winter and diffused in summer. Spathiphyllum will bloom in shade, but with undersized flowers that are few and far between.

Water: Keep the soil just moist, not soggy.

Special helps: Feed every two months from March to September with any complete soluble or liquid houseplant food.

When potbound, divide roots with a sharp knife after flowering. Pot up segments in standard potting mix to which you've added a handful of sand or perlite to create good drainage.

Leaves that turn brown at the edges and then yellow are simply aging; cut them off. When leaf tips yellow, the message is too much or not enough water, or insufficient food.

Strawberry saxifrage (strawberry geranium). This low-growing variegated plant produces dainty white flowers on tall stalks in summer. Undersides of the hairy leaves are reddish.

Light: Give bright, indirect sun, if possible.

Water: Let soil dry somewhat between waterings. And ensure good drainage to avoid waterlogged soil. Only moderate humidity is needed, so do not mist the foliage.

Special helps: To maintain the striking foliage colors, feed your strawberry saxifrage three times during the spring-summer active growth period.

Bright red aerial runners similar to those put out by fruit-bearing strawberries make propagation easy. In the spring, set 3-inch pots filled with moist potting soil next to the parent plant. Use a U-shaped wire to peg a runner close to a plantlet against the soil. When the plantlet has rooted, cut off the runner.

If red spider mites arrive on the scene, turn the plant on its side outdoors and hose the pests away.

Snowflake plant

Fishhook or pincushion cactus

Succulents.

Unique forms and sculpted shapes are the rule, not the exception, in this gigantic plant family. Succulent species number in the thousands, so there's endless diversity for you to discover. And since they are native to the desert, cactus and other succulents get along well in warm, dry homes.

The word succulents literally means "juicy plants"—ones that are capable of withstanding prolonged periods of drought. Some, such as cactus, actually store water; others have developed devices such as varnished leaf surfaces to cut down the need for water. Summer your succulents outdoors, placing them so they won't get intense full sun all day.

You can grow the fishhook or pincushion cactus *(Mammillaria aurihamata)* quite easily from seeds or from offsets. This cactus will flower when it's one year old and approximately one or two inches in diameter. In spring, the plant bears tiny yellow flowers, clustered in circles, which turn to red fruit in the fall.

Royal velvet *(Sulcorebutia rauschi)* seems to grow better on a graft. What looks like a stem in the picture at right is the stock or base cactus, *Cereus peruvianus.* Starting with one round, reddish-purple head, royal velvet produces offsets in a clump formation. The spines are short and blunt. Flowers, usually purple and red, appear in summer.

Neochilenia napina, the dwarf cactus pictured, can attain a diameter of one inch in two years. The flowers, showy in relation to the size of the plant, bloom in the fall and into the winter, lasting several days. Colors generally are pale yellow or a pale pink-salmon. Spines are harmless.

The *Agave victoriae-reginae* shown at right is 15 years old; this specimen will probably last until it's 20 or 21 years old. The plant flowers once, then gradually dies. Grow new ones from seed. Usually, the plants you find for sale are about three years old and stand about three inches high.

South African *Lithops bella* is but one of some 50 varieties of this plant species. The name "lithops" refers to the rock-like appearance of this odd little succulent. Flowers emerge from the central fissure of each pair of leaves.

Commonly called panda plant, *Kalanchoe tomentosa* puts out side branches in a bushy growth pattern as it matures. A dense matting of hairs covers the brown-edged leaves.

Partridge breast *(Aloe variegata)* grows in triangular rosettes and reaches six to nine inches at maturity. Supply bright light to obtain red flowers on foot-tall stems.

Donkey's tail *(Sedum morganianum)* needs more water than most succulents. Water lightly two or three times a week.

Sedum sieboldi, one of many sedums available, normally blooms in September and October, then goes dormant until March or April. It needs no water when resting.

Giant starfish flower *(Stapelia nobilis),* also called carrion-flower, belongs to the milkweed family. Flowering usually occurs in the fall, but can happen anytime during the growing season. The blooms appear only on new growth, so start new plants from cuttings every year or two.

Royal velvet

A dwarf cactus

Agave victoriae-reginae

Lithops bella

Kalanchoe tomentosa

Partridge breast

Donkey's tail

Echeveria Black Prince, a hybrid succulent, produces an abundant supply of flowers progressively over a period of several weeks. The container shown holds three mature plants, with 12-inch-high stalks growing out of rosettes.

Euphorbia lactea 'cristata' looks bizarre with its twisted, contorted growth habit. Propagate this succulent by cutting off a crest or "elkhorn," then rooting it to form a new plant.

Commonly called living rock cactus, *Ariocarpus fissuratus* often grows flat on the ground in native conditions. With watering, it gradually swells up to about a three-inch height.

Parodia mairanana, a free-flowering cactus native to Bolivia, grows easily from pups, or offsets, that cluster around its base. Nodes with spines grow in a spiral pattern from bottom to top, culminating in the one-inch bloom on top.

Light: Most succulents prefer south light. Some need protection from intense direct sun in the afternoon.

Water: Cactus and other succulents often need more water than you might think, especially during periods of active growth. Because water drains through the porous soil mix quickly, water every other week during spring and summer, depending on environmental conditions. In winter, reduce water drastically; maintain just enough to keep roots from drying out, but not enough to encourage new growth. The plants need this rest period; it's part of their natural cycle.

Special helps: Maintain good drainage. When potting, put rocks in the bottom of the container, preferably with gravel, broken pottery, or similar material with jagged edges. Don't use smooth rocks or pebbles. Fill the pot with planting mix to within one inch of the top edge. Cover the surface with aquarium gravel, small roof granules, or volcanic rock to reduce surface tension so water can soak right in.

The best potting mix for cactus and succulents consists of ⅓ humus, ⅓ perlite, and ⅓ washed sand (available at garden and building supply stores.) Don't use vermiculite in the mix—it retains too much moisture.

Feed cactus and other succulents frequently, but lightly. Choose a well-balanced analysis such as 10-10-5, either dry or liquid. This helps keep plants healthy and reduces the threat of disease or insect problems. If mealybugs start their white, cottony nests, isolate the infested plant and touch each pest with a cotton swab saturated with rubbing alcohol.

Propagate succulents by cuttings, seeds, or grafting. Start seeds in spring or early summer so they have a chance to grow before winter. Cutting is probably the easiest and most popular method. To root cuttings, use a combination of perlite (or peat or vermiculite) and sand, mixed half and half.

To propagate *Parodias*, cut off the offsets or pups that grow around the base of the plant. After you cut these off, put the start in a shady spot and allow to callus for a week or so. Then set it, cut side down, into the surface of the propagating mix, and start to water it. Some offsets come from the plant with roots started —in that case, dry the transplants for a day, or so to avoid fun-

Echeveria **Black Prince**

Euphorbia lactea 'cristata'

Living rock cactus

Parodia mairanana

gus, then treat them as you would established plants.

Propagate *Echeveria* Black Prince by taking a rosette leaf (or inflorescence leaf) and placing the tip in damp, loose dirt or sand, or a half-and-half mix of peat and sand. Place in a warm, damp, shady place until roots form—a few days to a week.

You can grow seeds of many cactus, including the *Mammillaria*. Scrape the seed from the fruit and dry it on a paper towel. Sprinkle the seeds on a low container of sterile potting mix and provide good drainage. Cover the seeds with a thin layer of coarse sand or gravel. To water, let the container absorb moisture from the bottom, so the water does not wash away the seeds. Cover the container with glass and a newspaper and place in a warm spot. The seeds will germinate best in shade; once they start to germinate, remove or lift the glass.

Grafting possibilities are almost limitless with cactus. The top section, or scion, usually retains its individual characteristics. Choose a stock, or under part, of a vigorous species of cactus. Using a clean, sharp knife, make a cut across the scion, halfway down, and cut the top off the stock. Trim back the skin on both the stock and the scion to make a better contact between the two vascular (soft tissue) rings. When the scion is in place, keep it in position with rubber bands going over the top and around the bottom of the pot. Remove the bands when the graft takes, in a day or so. The graft union should form quickly, within a week.

Christmas cactus

Crown-of-thorns

Christmas cactus *(Schlumbergera bridgesi)*. Although the showy Christmas cactus does belong to the cactus family, don't treat it the same way you do its thorny relatives.

Light: Unlike other cactuses, Christmas cactus resents too much direct summer sun. Diffuse south and west light.

Water: Christmas cactus is not a dry-soil plant that you can neglect for weeks on end like some of its kin. Give it porous soil and even watering during most of the year.

Special helps: Now, here's the trick to obtain flashy blooms in December. Withhold water in the fall for a month. Resume cautiously in November, but don't let the stems get flabby from overwatering. From October on, keep the plant where it's cool at night—60 to 65° F.

Propagate by cutting shoots back from tips at the second joint. Stick the cuttings in a moist perlite-peat mix. Water sparingly at first so the stems don't rot. Pot up when rooted.

Crown-of-thorns *(Euphorbia splendens)*. This succulent comes in a flower choice of pinkish white, rose, red, or coral.

Light: Grow crown-of-thorns in medium, filtered light.

Water: Water only when the soil surface dries out.

Special helps: Propagate in spring or early summer. Dry cuttings for several days before inserting in moist, coarse sand or perlite to root. Pot up in regular houseplant soil.

Please don't pet the plants!
Place succulents such as donkey's tail and jade plant where people or animals won't brush against them accidentally. The leaves fall off at the slightest pressure. If this happens, just stick them, stubby end down, into the soil the parent plant is growing in, or into any porous rooting mixture.

Trileaf wonder

Summer outings. *Many house-plants benefit from spending the summer outdoors in the fresh air in a filtered-light location protected from damaging winds.*

Sink the pots in the ground if you prefer, but don't cover the pot rims. Give the sunken pots a half-turn occasionally during the summer to prevent roots from growing through the drainage holes and taking firmer anchor in the surrounding soil.

Before returning the plants to the house in the fall, check them carefully for plant pests.

Trileaf wonder (*Syngonium podophyllum;* arrow-head plant). Arrow-shaped leaves give trileaf wonder its nickname. A slow-growing relative of the philodendron, this plant sports slender, ruffly leaflets ranging in size up to five inches. Coloration of syngonium varies, with some green, some white, a lot of mottling but with green leaf margins.

Keep trileaf wonder within bounds by pinching new shoots to the height desired—the long, willowy stems can reach several feet. If yours are in pots, train the tall stems to a stick wrapped with moist sphagnum. Some varieties of syngonium work well in hanging baskets. Small plants will thrive in a terrarium, but will crowd out their neighbors unless you keep pruning them back to moderate size.

Light: Trileaf wonder isn't fussy about light. A sunny east window or a bright north window provides ideal light. The plant will do well placed away from a window provided the nearby walls are a light color that reflects indirect sunlight well. Avoid hot, direct sun during summer.

Water: This plant loves moisture and medium humidity. Keep the soil evenly moist, but not soggy. If you've provided a moss-covered support for the willowy stems to climb, water the moss often enough that it doesn't dry out completely. During the home-heating season, mist foliage every morning.

Special helps: Apply a houseplant fertilizer not more than once a month during spring and summer.

Start new plants easily from stem cuttings (see page 88 for instructions). When rooted, pot up the starts, using a standard houseplant soil mixture. Or, make your own of equal parts loam soil, peat, and perlite or sharp sand.

Protect trileaf wonder from rapid temperature changes. Don't allow the plant to become potbound—knock the plant out of the pot to check for crowded roots. Shift to a pot that's an inch larger in diameter, if necessary. When your trileaf wonder becomes leggy and unsightly, take several stem cuttings before discarding the parent plant.

Umbrella plant (*Cyperus alternifolius*). The feathery top growth of the umbrella plant complements the older, coarser foliage. A dwarf relative of the 10-foot-tall papyrus, *C. alternifolius* reaches four feet. Its variety 'gracilis' attains 12 to 18 inches; 'nana,' 12 inches; 'diffusus,' 6 to 10 inches. Look for umbrella plant at counters devoted to terrarium plants. It does well in terrarium culture.

Light: Keep this plant several feet from the window if you grow it in sunlight. It will settle for bright, diffused light (reflection from a light-colored wall).

Water: A true daughter of the Nile, umbrella plant likes constant moisture. The pot can even stand in a saucer of water.

Special helps: Feed with any complete soluble or liquid houseplant fertilizer every two weeks during the active growth period of spring through summer.

When clumps grow too large to suit you, divide the roots and pot up the segments in separate pots. Add sand to regular houseplant potting mixture to make it porous.

If mealybugs attack by erecting their white, cottony fortresses, annihilate them by touching each pest with a cotton swab saturated with rubbing alcohol.

Umbrella plant

Waffle plant *(Hemigraphis)*. (See the photo of this plant on page 59 with sanchezia.) Waffle plant spreads out, making it an attractive groundcover for planters. You can also grow it in individual pots or hanging baskets.

The waffle plant features extremely dark green leaves with a metallic luster and reddish undersides. Leaf veins tend to be deeply set with some puckering or waffling effect. Leaf edges are serrated or toothed.

Several young plants set in a container will give a fuller immediate impact than will one plant. Grow waffle plant for its unusual foliage rather than the small, white flowers.

Light: Give bright light, such as in a north or east window.

Water: Waffle plant performs best when the soil is kept slightly moist. Avoid letting the soil dry out too much. The plant likes high humidity; mist foliage each morning.

Special helps: Apply houseplant fertilizer not more than once a month. Waffle plant propagates itself naturally by rooting along the low-growing stems where leaf nodes touch moist, peaty soil. Sever the connecting stem and transplant the young starts; or take three- to four-inch tip cuttings. Remove the lowest pair of leaves and stick the cutting into a sterile, moist rooting medium such as vermiculite (see page 88). When rooted, pot up, using a standard houseplant potting mixture.

Zebra plant

Zebra plant *(Aphelandra)*. This plant, with its boldly striped foliage, belongs in every plant collection. Although the individual blooms last only a short time, the dramatic yellow color show continues for several weeks, since new flowers come out to replace those that fade as the spike elongates.

Light: Keep your zebra plant in bright, indirect light. Avoid full sun, which will burn the foliage.

Water: Add water when the soil surface feels almost dry. Leaves usually are stiff (they sag a little when the plant is in bloom); if they become flexible, water thoroughly.

Special helps: After flowering, zebra plant may drop its bottom leaves and become leggy and unsightly. If this happens, the best, and easiest, course of action is to start a new plant with a tip cutting. Use a sharp knife to cut off a four-to six-inch growing tip just below the point where a leaf joins the stem (roots develop best at this point). Remove lower leaves and stick stem in moist coarse sand or perlite-peat mix. Water and keep in a cool, light location. When rooted, pot up the new plant in a regular houseplant soil mixture.

Clockwise from top left: amaryllis, daffodils, crocus, tulips, hyacinths.

Bulbs

Even when it's cold and blowing outside, you can have something colorful and growing inside by "forcing" spring bulbs. In many cases, all you do is buy prepared bulbs, add water, and enjoy the show. Others need a little room in your refrigerator, closet, or basement for a few weeks.

Forcing is a technique that speeds up the normal blooming time of bulb plants—from six or seven months to less than four months. Bulb selection, of course, is critical. Choose bulbs that are firm, plump, and free of bruises and blemishes. The larger the bulb you use, the better your results will be.

If you're not going to pot your bulbs immediately, you can store them for several weeks on open racks in a well-ventilated room. The temperature should range from 50 to 60° F.

Select a pot that is at least twice as tall as the bulbs you're using. This way, you're sure there'll be room for good root development. It doesn't matter what the pot is made of; just be sure it has a drainage hole. Wash the pot thoroughly and place a shard (a piece of broken clay pot) over the hole to keep the soil from draining out.

Your potting soil should be porous enough for water to drain through easily. A good mix includes equal parts of loamy potting soil, peat moss, and sand or vermiculite. Don't reuse soil that already has been used to force bulbs. Fertilizing is unnecessary because the bulb has all the nutrients and fertilizer the plant needs.

To pot the bulbs, first fill the pot half-full with the potting mixture, but don't pack it down. Then, place the bulbs on top of soil —press them down slightly, just enough to make sure they'll stay in place. If you press too hard you may damage the bulb and hinder root development. For the best looking results when the plants bloom, fill the pot with as many bulbs as possible. In a six-inch-diameter pot, for example, plant four to six tulips or daffodils, three hyacinths, or 10 crocus. In an eight-inch-diameter pot, plant six to eight tulips or daffodils, four or five hyacinths, and about 15 crocus. Don't allow the bulbs to touch in the pot—leave at least a pencil-width between them.

Fill the pot with the remaining soil, filtering it down between the bulbs. Cover until just the bulb tips are visible. Tamp it down and water. You may wish to label each pot you plant with the date planted and the name of variety or bulb. On tulips and other bulbs that need cold storage, add date they can be taken out (see chart on page 72).

With some bulbs (see chart) your next step is to simulate the effect winter has by placing the potted bulbs in cold storage. An unheated basement or root cellar is ideal—the garage, a refrigerator, or an outdoor shed are other possibilities. Make sure temperatures are in the 35° to 50° F. range and that they

Lilies-of-the-valley

71

PLANT	POTTING INSTRUCTIONS	COMMENTS
Amaryllis	**Buy treated bulb that's ready to flower. If not preplanted, plant in a six-inch pot, leaving half the bulb above soil. Set one per pot.**	*This warm-climate native likes warmth, so set potted bulb in a sunny window or in a warm room with good light. Water often enough to keep the soil evenly moist. As the big stems push up, you may need to tie them to stake for support. Flowers can be red, pink, white, or coral; some are striped.*
Tulips	**Plant six bulbs in a six-inch clay pot, setting each bulb with its nose showing above the soil level, an inch between each.**	*After bulbs are planted in a pot, water thoroughly, then set pot in the refrigerator for 12 weeks; water weekly to keep soil moist. Next, move the pot to a cool, dark closet or basement location for two weeks, continuing to water. Put them in a warm, sunny spot; they'll bloom in five weeks.*
Daffodils	**Set six daffodil bulbs in an eight-inch pot. Be sure pot has good drainage at bottom. Plant bulbs so their necks peek out of soil.**	*After you've set daffodils in pot, water soil well, then put pot in refrigerator for eight to 12 weeks. (To judge progress, water soil, then tap out to check roots–if roots fill bottom of pot, bulbs are ready for the next step.) When cold treatment is over, put pot in a sunny window.*
Crocus	**Plant ten corms in a six-inch pot. Crowd the corms to get better display, but be sure to leave at least a pencil's width between them.**	*Water the pot after you've planted crocus, then place pot in a refrigerator or cool closet for eight weeks, keeping the soil moist during this period. When this pre-flowering treatment is finished, place pot in cool room where the light is strong. Plants will flower in four weeks.*
Hyacinths	**Use one bulb for a hyacinth vase if you grow in water; use three bulbs in a six-inch pot if you grow hyacinths in soil.**	*If you use a hyacinth vase, fill vase with water, then put in refrigerator for seven weeks. If you pot in soil, water pot, then put in refrigerator for seven weeks. With both, remove from cold at the end of the treatment period, put in partial sun one week, then move to a spot with full sun.*
Paper-white narcissus	**Start with a six-inch-diameter, pebble-filled bowl and wedge four bulbs among the pebbles. Add water to cover bases of bulbs.**	*Store planted bowl in a cool, dark closet or basement for two weeks, replenishing the water in bowl as necessary. After this time period, bring bowl to the sunniest location you have. The flower spikes will shoot up in a hurry. And the fragrant blooms should open in three weeks.*
Iris	**Set two or three rhizomes in a ten-inch pot, each just below the surface of the soil. Start with pretreated roots, or treat them.**	*To simulate winter for rhizomes, put planted pot in refrigerator for ten weeks (skip this step if you buy pretreated rhizomes). After this period, move pot directly to maximum light at average room temperature. Water often, both in storage and later. Flowers come in eight weeks.*
Lilies-of-the-valley	**Buy cold-treated pips; they're usually sold already packed in a moist, fibrous growing medium. Slip into new bowl if you prefer.**	*Water the growing medium thoroughly, then set the pot in a location where light is strong (but not where pot can get direct sun). There's little else you need do, except to check the water situation daily to be sure the growing medium stays moist, not soggy. Expect blooms in three weeks.*

never drop below freezing. Cover the pots with other pots or put them in a covered box so no light reaches them. Be sure to water regularly—keep the soil evenly moist and pour off excess water that drains through the pot.

In about eight to twelve weeks (depending on the bulb type), check the pots for root development. If roots are visible through drainage holes and the stems are about two or three inches tall, the bulbs are ready for an artificially created spring. Move them into a cool (60° F.) room for about two weeks—keep them out of light, and water them regularly as you did in cold storage.

In two weeks the plants should have buds. Move them into a room at normal house temperatures (not to exceed 72° F.) where they will bloom shortly. To prolong the bloom period, keep the plants out of direct sun and away from heating ducts and radiators. Put them in a cool room at night. Water regularly.

To get your bulbs to bloom in January, you should pot them in early October. For February bloom, pot in October or November; for March bloom, pot in mid-November.

Tulip tip. When potting tulip bulbs, place the flat side of the bulb toward the outside of the pot. The first broad leaf comes from the flat side—if they all face out, they'll form a foliage border around edge of the pot.

Iris

Paper-white narcissus

Terrarium plants

A petite forest under glass

Gardening in a large glass bowl or other glass container is as appealing and rewarding for the beginner as for the experienced gardener. When properly planted and watered, a terrarium will remain beautiful for many months, and with very little care—a boon for the casual gardener.

The difference between an attractive, well-ordered arrangement and a chaotic conglomeration revolves around planning. When deciding on the approach you want to take, remember that the star performers are the plants. So, leave space between them so each can show as an individual. And to put the landscape in perspective, buy at least one plant that's taller than the others to act as a miniature tree. Other ways to add interest to your setting include using rocks or pieces of driftwood and variegated-leaved plants.

Eight little plants are skillfully arranged in the terrarium at right. Duplicates of the plants used, set in the upper left corner, show how they looked when bought—all were purchased in small-size plastic pots. Mist and check for watering needs topless terrariums such as this every week. If covered, once-a-month watering is fine.

Shopping for your miniature garden can be much of the fun in starting a terrarium. Most plant specialty shops have sections devoted to terrarium-size plants, which helps a great deal. The tendency is to buy too many plants, and if you buy them, you'll probably put them all in whether they are needed or not. So, before buying, arrange your selections on a countertop as you visualize them in your container.

Small African violets, baby's tears, artillery plants, aluminum plants, creeping figs, coleus, small Chinese evergreens, English ivy, fittonias, little ferns, Hahn's sansevierias, small aralias, impatiens, mosses, peperomias, and wax-plants are just a few specimens that adapt beautifully to terrarium culture. In large-scale terrariums, you can put everblooming begonias, caladiums, pickaback plants, prayer plants, and non-vining philodendrons to good use.

Take a little extra time to give plant roots a healthy environment by layering soil ingredients. Start with a thin layer of charcoal across the bottom, and top with a half inch of gravel. Then, put in an inch or more of potting soil. (An option that adds to the appearance of any terrarium is to line the sides of the container with a thin layer of sphagnum moss before adding the soil ingredients.) Before you plant, water lightly two or three times until the soil is moist. Finally, set plants in their places after digging little holes large enough for their soil balls.

Ingredients for a terrarium

A window bottle garden

Water plants

Where water gardening is concerned, it doesn't matter what color your thumb is. There's little more involved than filling a small container with water and sticking the cut end of a stem in it. For such a simple procedure, the results can be outstanding.

Once you have the cuttings in the water, Mother Nature takes over. Roots soon appear along the submerged stems, followed shortly by new leaves at the top. Another beauty of water culture is that after-care is almost as simple as the initial step. For best results, it's wise to change the water every week or so to keep it sweet and fresh. Add a few grains of soluble plant food or a couple of drops of a liquid type in the water after each change. If there's excessive root growth, simply cut back the roots or pot the plants in soil. Pot up carefully, as water-grown roots tend to be a bit brittle and may snap off if handled roughly.

Supplement the color in your display by putting a tiny bouquet of summer flowers in one of the bright bottles, or force some flowering branches for early spring blossoms.

When choosing plants, select species that perform reliably without soil. Count on English, Swedish, and grape ivies, golden pothos, coleus, Chinese evergreen, dracena, trileaf wonder, tradescantia, philodendron, bloodleaf, and croton. Some plants flourish best on a sunny window shelf; others do better in a ceramic vase on a living room lamp table. Move your cuttings around until you find the combination that's compatible. *Here are some fine plants that respond to water culture:*

Dracena, also known as corn plant, likes filtered sunlight. Take 12- to 15-inch cuttings with leafy heads. Or, try another type of dracena called the inch plant. It roots quickly and its creeping growth drapes over the sides of the container.

Philodendron offers a variety of leaf sizes and shapes. You can trim the plant to keep the vining growth compact or let it spread. Give filtered light.

Grape ivy grows rapidly to fill its areas with deep green, grapelike leaves. It likes bright light, but no direct sun.

Chinese evergreen offers its comparatively large leaves held on firm, upright stems to give variety to your windowsill bottle garden. Since it will grow well in dim light, you can set it some distance from a window.

Coleus, probably the easiest plant to root, contributes its bright foliage to your collection. It can survive some direct sun, but its color is best in diffused light.

Sweet potatoes are the most responsive of all plants to water culture. Their lush vining growth literally cascades from the tuber that's half submerged in water. With very little care, you'll have a specimen plant in just a few weeks. Give it bright light, but no direct sun. Prune the vines if they grow out of bounds.

Brighten your window garden by putting some of your cuttings in colorful glass containers. Roots of some plants do even better when light rays are filtered by the tinted glass. Turn containers occasionally so plants don't lean too much. Tidiness is most important for the looks of your little glass garden, so keep dead leaves trimmed off and keep the glass sparkling.

Holiday plants

Christmas gift plants—azalea, Christmas pepper, Christmas cherry, cyclamen, Rieger elatior begonia, poinsettia, and others—will stay attractive long after the holiday season is over, provided you know the conditions and care they require. For example, all require bright light—preferably sunlight—during the day and in a cool room (about 65° F.) at night. And all need watering before the soil is dry to the touch. Removing the metal foil the plant was wrapped in at the greenhouse or punching a hole in the bottom of the foil contributes to the long-lasting beauty of the plants by allowing for adequate drainage. Be sure also to put a saucer under each pot and pour water until it runs out the drainage hole (then empty water from the saucer).

Now, let's take a look at the particulars of caring for each of the plants shown. The blossoms on an **azalea,** upper left, will last longer if plants have bright light in daytime and cool (below 65° F.) night temperatures. Keep a constant, even moisture supply—flowers will wilt and die prematurely if soil becomes too dry. Soak the pot in water occasionally so moisture will penetrate to center of pot. Remove old flowers as they fade. To keep your plant growing, fertilize with acid-type azalea fertilizer every few weeks from the time the flowers fade in the spring until new buds form; do not fertilize while plant is flowering.

Christmas pepper and Christmas cherry (lower left) are readily available and reasonably priced during the Yule season —the plants' attractive foliage, and colorful fruits and blooms make cheerful additions to any holiday decor. To prolong their beauty, give plants bright light and cool temperatures (60° F. at night). An occasional mist spray of water keeps them looking their best. Treat pepper plants (foreground) as annuals—throw them away when they become unattractive. You can dry peppers and use them as seasoning, but watch out—they're hot! Both Christmas peppers and Christmas cherries are easy to grow from seed. Plant in pots in the spring and put them outdoors in a sunny spot. Move inside before frost, and you can have fruits by Christmas.

Water the **cyclamen** (opposite, upper right) around the edges of the pot because water in the crown may cause rot. You can also set plant in a dish of water and let it soak up the moisture. Never let the soil dry out while the plant is in flower or leaves will turn yellow. Leaf yellowing as well as bud blasting also may occur if the night temperature is too high (above 70° F.) or if the plant is not getting enough daylight. It will do best in bright, indirect light. Cyclamen plants should last a month or more in your home. Fertilize every two weeks for longer growth.

The **Rieger elatior begonia** (lower right) thrives under good light and with average care. It has above-average lasting quality and is characterized by its dark green foliage and

Azalea

Christmas pepper and Christmas cherry

orange, red, or salmon-coral flowers. To lengthen the blooming time to several weeks, select a plant in the half-open bud stage. It will do best if you keep it barely moist. You can move these begonias outdoors in warm weather. Sink pots in a semi-shaded flower bed or use as a potted plant on your patio. Grow in a soil that has a generous amount of peat moss.

Probably the most popular of all Christmas plants, the **poinsettia** (below) is familiar to everyone. Newest varieties last longer than ever and are also less sensitive to drafts and temperature extremes. However, temperatures below 60° F. or above 75° F. will shorten the life of the colorful bracts. The true flowers of poinsettia are the tiny greenish yellow nubs in the centers of the bracts—which may be white or pink as well as the popular red.

Poinsettias do best when they receive at least four hours of direct sunlight in a draft-free location. Cut back plants in late spring after flowering and repot in fresh potting soil. Your poinsettia may survive as a foliage plant for years after you purchase it. It's possible, but difficult to bring it into color a second or third time. The plant will flower only if you give it an alternation of light and at least 14 hours of darkness each day for six weeks. Do this in September and October for bloom by Christmas.

Norfolk Island pine (pictured on page 43) is often used as a miniature Christmas tree. Named for the tiny island in the South Pacific where it grows wild, Norfolk Island pine does well in bright, indirect, or filtered light; in winter it can stand full sun. Water generously as long as drainage is adequate.

Cyclamen

Rieger elatior begonia

Poinsettia

Green thumb basics

At one time, the luck a person had (or didn't have) growing house-plants was explained away by any number of seat-of-the-pants theories. Today, that's all changed. If your plants don't flourish, they have fallen victim to one or more of the following: too much or too little light, water, or food; too low or too high humidity; poor potting soil; too high or too low temperatures; or insect and disease problems. Inspect your plants regularly for the first signs of trouble. Safeguard your plants—and make your plant-growing experiences more satisfying—by reading the basics that follow.

Pots and potting

Select your container. The traditional clay pot comes close to being the ideal houseplant container. Because clay is relatively porous, you run less chance of waterlogging than you do if you use a ceramic or plastic con-

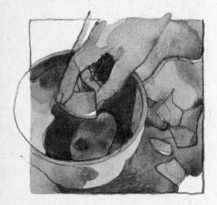

tainer. All of the standard-design clay pots have bottom drainage holes that let excess water escape.

Old-fashioned clay containers are made in sizes ranging from the minute, two-inch starting pots to jumbo containers large enough to hold a potted tree. The classic style has a depth equal to the top diameter (bulb and azalea pans are not as deep as they are wide).

Decoratively, it's hard to top the effect you get from the earthy, terra-cotta color of clay pots. The tone harmonizes well with green plants.

Plastic pots are easier to ship since they're lightweight and not subject to breakage; hence, plastic pots usually cost less

than their clay counterparts. And you can get almost any size pot you wish in plastic—some come equipped with attached saucers. However, a plastic pot doesn't permit respiration through the sides; you have to be careful not to overwater plants potted in containers that aren't porous.

The same drawbacks apply to *glazed containers* too. Also, many decorative ceramic containers and jardinieres don't have bottom drainage holes, so the risks of waterlogging are increased. Many houseplant fanciers overcome this difficulty by potting plants in clay or plastic containers, then placing pots into the decorative jardinieres.

You can plant directly into a drainless ceramic container if you add a layer of gravel or pebbles in the bottom of the pot. This helps prevent trouble, but you still have to be careful not to waterlog the soil and roots and lose plants because of excess moisture.

Why use a shard? A shard is a broken piece of pottery, usually a fragment of a broken flowerpot, (left). If you don't have smashed pottery, you can use a small square of screening or a soft drink bottle cap.

The purpose of the shard is to cover the hole in the bottom of the pot. Why have a hole in the bottom of a pot and then cover it up? The hole is there so excess water can escape, and the shard keeps the soil in the

pot from washing out as the surplus water drains away.

Condition new pots. Before you use a new clay pot, take time to condition it. Immerse it completely in a pail of water and leave it there until all bubbling and hissing stop. (The hissing is barely audible, but you will hear it if you lean close to the water.) Once the sound stops, the pot is ready for planting.

Why go through all this? It's recommended because clay absorbs moisture, and the newer the clay, the more it absorbs. A new pot not conditioned can rob water from the soil it holds.

This explains why some newly potted plants wilt, in spite of correct watering. If the pot has been conditioned properly, wilting will be minimal.

Don't condition plastic or glazed ceramic containers—they don't absorb moisture.

Repotting time. Keep watch for signs that a plant needs to be repotted. Sometimes, the need

is obvious. Any plant growing in a two- or three-inch pot makes a likely candidate. If the plant is growing spindly, or not growing at all, the trouble may well be pot size. Change to a four-inch container.

Repotting is in order, too, if you buy a small plant and discover you have to water it daily because the soil mix is so porous it won't hold moisture.

Repot any plant whose roots have begun to grow through the drainage hole.

Check any plant that has been in the same container for two or more years; it may be root-bound. Turn pot and plant upside down. Grasp base of stem between your fingers and tap the rim of pot to remove plant (left). If the soil ball is filled with roots, repot the rootbound plant in a slightly larger container.

If you've received a gift planter containing four or five young plants, repot each in its own pot (right) before they start crowding each other to death.

How to pot a plant. Select the right size container. Generally,

shift a plant to a container no more than an inch bigger than its former pot. If you're potting cuttings or offshoots, a four- or five-inch pot will suffice.

Use good-quality soil that's *moist;* it shouldn't be either soggy wet or completely dry (keep soil in a closed plastic bag to hold moisture in). You can buy potting soil, or mix your own. For the majority of houseplants, a mix of ⅓ sand, ⅓ leaf mold or peat, and ⅓ garden soil works well. Succulents, orchids, bromeliads, and African violets prefer mixtures with different proportions, as noted on the pages dealing with these plants.

Now, follow these simple steps.
1. If the pot has a drainage hole, put a piece of shard over it. If the pot is holeless, put an inch-deep layer of gravel in the bottom.
2. Gently knock plant out of its present pot, holding plant in one hand and the pot in the other. Retain as much soil around the roots as possible.
3. Hold plant in the center of the pot (left); the bottom of the stem should be about an inch below the pot rim. Fill space under and around roots with potting soil, firming soil down as you work.
4. Water the newly potted plant well, then set it in a spot away from direct sun for a week or two.

Watering

More plants perish from over-watering than from underwatering. The reason: excessively wet soil crowds out the oxygen needed by the roots, and the roots can't support the leaves if they don't have oxygen. Even plants that require a lot of water will die if kept soggy wet.

The two coleus above were the same size and shape when potted. The one on the left was watered only when the soil surface started to dry. The other received daily soakings, with the result that some leaves lost their luster, others dropped, and growth was stunted.

When and how much to water depend upon various factors. For example, if your home is arid, you'll have to water more frequently than if you have high humidity. Plants in small pots will need water more often than those in large pots. A plant in bloom needs extra water.

Follow this golden rule: when you water, be thorough. Supply enough to moisten the soil all the way to the bottom of the pot. Thorough watering once a week serves better than shallow watering every other day. Use only unsoftened water on plants.

Some plants grow only in water (waterlilies), some grow in either water or soil (Chinese evergreen), but no plant growing in soil will thrive if you let its roots stand in water.

When you water thoroughly—as you should—the water should drain through the hole in the bottom of the pot and accumulate in the saucer below. The important thing to remember is to empty the saucer. Don't let the pot stand in this excess water.

If you have plants potted in clay or plastic containers and set in ceramic overpots, lift up the inner pot after watering and empty water from the jardiniere.

Every month or two, water your plants by immersion to be sure that all of the soil gets watered. In between, follow your regular routine with watering can, pitcher, or glass when soil surface feels dry to the touch.

To immerse a plant, fill a pail or dishpan with water deep enough to just come over the rim of pot. Set pot under water and leave it until bubbling stops. The time this takes depends on size of soil mass and how dry it is.

Then, remove the pot from water and set it in a sink to drain completely. Meanwhile, you might mist and clean the foliage.

Don't go away and leave a plant immersed for longer than necessary. Too much water over a long period of time prevents oxygen from getting to roots.

An easy way to water. Double-pot if you're a forgetful gardener (see drawing above). Set a potted plant inside a second pot two sizes larger, and line space between pots with sphagnum moss. Keep moss moist by soaking it once a week. (The moisture will seep through the inner clay pot wall to provide even moisture.)

Consider the pot when you water. Clay pots present the

fewest dangers at watering time. Clay absorbs moisture from the soil, thus minimizing the danger of waterlogging at bottom of the pot. When the soil surface in a clay pot feels dry, you can safely assume the plant needs water.

The plastic pot often has a drainage hole so excess water can escape. But since the plastic isn't porous, the water held by the soil doesn't evaporate as fast as from a porous clay pot. The soil surface can feel dry while the soil at the bottom of the pot still is wet. Anticipate this circumstance, and water plants in plastic pots less often.

Ceramic containers are the most risky to use. Solid bottoms hold excess water. Water just enough to moisten roots. You may have to water more frequently, but not thoroughly.

Increase the humidity. Daily misting of foliage is recommended for plants, such as ferns, that thrive in high humidity (see drawing at left). Mist in the morning so plants will dry off and not stand damp overnight.

You also can provide moisture in the air around the plants by using a pebble tray (see drawing at left, bottom). Fill a waterproof tray with pebbles or pea gravel and set your potted plants atop the rocks. Keep water in the tray to a level below the top of the pebbles or gravel.

Hot weather tip. When the mercury soars, plants give off a lot of moisture that you should replace. If some of your plants are summering outdoors, they also have to cope with drying winds, which are equally rough on foliage. So check plants daily and water those that need it—let the moist ones alone. Plants by open windows are more subject to drying out quickly. Air conditioning decreases the humidity; compensate with extra watering.

Vacation plant care

Those lightweight plastic bags from the cleaners make perfect greenhouse environments to hold plants for up to three weeks while you go on vacation.

Move plants out of direct sunlight. If you take a winter vacation, turn heat down to about 60° F.

Tape the top of the cleaner bag closed. Get bamboo stakes (inexpensive at variety stores or plant shops) that are taller than your plant and stick three or four in the pot to hold the bag away from the foliage. (Cardboard taped to the tops of the stakes will stop punctures.)

Water the plant as usual. Don't soak it or mist the foliage; too much moisture causes mold in the airtight bag. Place the pot in the bag (see the drawing below) and tie the plastic so no air or moisture will escape. Put more than one plant in a bag if they aren't crowded.

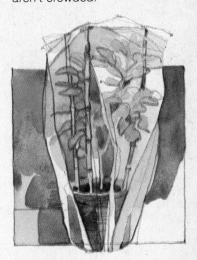

If you have a plant too large to cover completely, water it as usual and bag just the container. Tape or tie the bag to the trunk or stem so you'll have no moisture leakage. Half-bagging isn't as effective as putting the whole plant in a closed system, but it will support plant for two weeks.

Feeding plants

Don't overfertilize! A little plant food goes a long way—too much can burn the roots and kill the plant. Always follow directions on the plant food label.

Let new plants adjust to their move to your home for six to eight weeks before feeding. Most established plants benefit from light feeding once a month during their active growth in spring and summer, but stop feeding them in fall and winter when they go into their normal dormancy period.

Don't assume that any sickly plant will benefit from a dose of plant food. The plant might be ailing from too little light, too much or too little water, or too dry an atmosphere.

If nitrogen is lacking, the symptoms are yellow color in new leaves and lack of vigor in new growth. Similar symptoms appear from gas fumes, too much water, and too little light. But when these are the culprit, the mature bottom leaves turn yellow, not the new leaves.

Commercial fertilizers always indicate on the package the proportions of nutrients they contain. When you see three figures, such as 6-8-6, the first represents nitrogen; the second, phosphorus; and the third, potash. Buy food specially designed for houseplants so the balance of these important nutrients will be correct for container-grown plants.

Plant food comes in powdered, granulated, tablet, and

liquid form. Always moisten the soil before applying food. The timed-release fertilizers give plants nutrients over an extended period.

Greenery cleanup

Remove dust from plant leaves periodically; otherwise, plants can't breathe or grow properly.

You can clean many plants quickly by putting them under your shower. Use only luke-warm, unsoftened water. When finished, let plants drip-dry before taking them back to their accustomed positions. If chemical residue in the water leaves white spots, remove them with a clean, soft cloth.

Don't use a waxy leaf polish to clean plants, as it clogs the pores. If you want to renew sheen, rub the leaves gently between your index finger and thumb. Or, apply skim milk gently over the upper sides of the leaves, and use a dry pad of cotton to remove the milk residue. Do only a few leaves at a time, as you must remove the residue before it dries.

Remove dust from hairy-leaved plants such as African violet by rubbing gently with a dry cotton swab or pipe cleaner (see drawing at left).

Insect/disease problems

If your plant's been well fed, sunned, humidified, and watered . . . and still looks mangy—check it for these plant plagues.

Mealybugs. White, cottony blobs on any part of a plant indicate the presence of mealybugs. Check undersides of leaves and stems—the pests gravitate to parts of the plant that are not exposed to the sun. Dab each bug with a cotton swab dipped in rubbing alcohol. Afterwards, rinse the leaves with tepid, unsoftened water.

Red spider mites. These tiny bugs feed underneath the leaves, spinning fine webs along veins and leaves. They thrive in a desert-dry environment and leave a plant with a

gray webby look and anemic foliage.

If you notice the problem before the plant is too far gone, take it outside, lay it on its side, and blast the undersides of leaves with a hose spray. Or, lather up a pan of lukewarm water and soap (not detergent). Cover the top of the pot with foil to hold the dirt, upend the plant, and swish the foliage through the suds. Rinse well with clear water. A weekly bath may be needed to completely eradicate the varmints. Mist foliage daily to discourage resettlement.

Aphids. These insects, commonly greenish white or black, cluster in the open where they're readily detected. Attack with the warm, soapy water wash and clear rinse recommended for red spider mites. Successive generations may hatch, so be prepared to re-treat the plant to achieve final victory.

Scale. Another common sucking pest, scale especially likes ferns and citrus plants. The young scale is small, crawly, and hard to detect until it digs into the stems or leaf veins and grows a hard, brown shell.

No wash or water spray will dislodge these small barnacles, so push them off with a soft toothbrush or wet cloth.

Rot. The only indoor plant disease you're likely to see is an infection called "damping off" in seedlings and "stem rot" in older plants. This plague came with the soil your plants are in, and you can't kill the organisms without losing the plant. There's no cure, so start with a sterilized potting mixture to avoid the problem.

Houseplant propagation

Plants need to be renewed when they get too big or leggy, or if a part of the plant starts to die back. So, if you have a plant that qualifies for any of these reasons, or if you just want more plants, it's time to propagate.

Root division. Division (see the drawing below) is the easiest way to increase clump-forming plants such as self-heading philodendron, Boston fern, asparagus fern, aspidistra, Chinese evergreen, maranta, pandanus, peperomia, and sansevieria.

The day before you want to divide a plant, water the soil ball thoroughly. The next day, turn pot upside down, supporting the plant with one hand. Tap the pot rim on a table, and slip the plant out of the pot. Shake soil from the roots so you can see possible points for division.

Generally, you can pull plant sections apart with a few gentle tugs. But occasionally, the roots are tough and hopelessly intertwined. Then, you'll need

to take a sharp knife and cut the sections apart. This treatment may sound like mayhem, but the divisions will survive if you get each of them potted up quickly.

Water the new divisions daily for at least a week, and keep them out of direct sun for at least two weeks while they adjust.

Stem cuttings. The most common way to propagate is by taking stem cuttings. While most stem cuttings root easily in water, water-grown roots are more brittle and more apt to break off in potting than roots started in sand or perlite mixes.

To take a stem cutting, cut off a four-to six-inch growing tip with a sharp knife. Make the cut just below the point where a leaf joins the stem. (Roots develop best at this node.)

Remove the lower leaves so the bottom two inches of stem are bare. (Leaves left on could rot and eventually cause the cutting to die.) Dip the cut end in a root-promoting powder (see the drawing above) if you wish to speed up the propagating process. Insert cutting in a container of moist, coarse sand or perlite-peat mix. Water and keep in a cool, light location.

A greenhouse-type environment will promote humidity and encourage growth, so if desired, cover the cutting and container with a clear plastic bag; insert stakes in the pot to hold the tent away from the foliage.

After three or four weeks, remove cutting gently to check for roots. When roots have formed, pot up the new plant.

Air layering. Some large plants with woody stems drop their lower leaves if grown too long in dim light, or if overwatered. The remedy for this: restore them to their former attractiveness by means of air layering.

To air layer, make a cut partway through the stem at a severe angle, and insert a wooden match to keep the cut open. Mold a baseball-size wad

of wet sphagnum moss around the cut, enclose in a sheet of plastic, and tie the plastic at top and bottom (see the drawing).

Keep the moss moist. In four weeks, the moss ball will be

lined with new roots. Cut off the stem below these new roots and pot up. Shorten the remaining stem to three or four inches and continue to water the old potted roots. New growth will sprout on the short stub in time.

Runners and offsets. Plants that send out aerial runners and form new plantlets couldn't be easier to propagate. When these plants grew in their natural settings, the weight of each developing plantlet would bring it down until it came in contact with moist soil, then it would root. When these species are grown as houseplants, you have to imitate nature at propagating time and provide a nearby soil-filled pot for offsets.

When a new plant forms, fill a five-inch pot with a soil mix that's half peat moss and half sand. Water mix well at planting time. Using a hairpin or a bent loop of wire, pin the plantlet to the soil in the small pot as illustrated above. Don't sever the runner leading to the parent.

Roots will form in four or

five weeks. Keep the soil mix uniformly moist during this critical time.

Gently feel the base of the new plant to see if it's firmly anchored in the soil. When the new plant holds fast under light pressure from your fingers, you know it's rooted. You can then sever the runner.

Leaf cuttings. African violets, gloxinias, and a number of

begonias bear leaves that are capable of producing roots. To start these leaves in water, fill a jar or glass with water, cover top with foil, and pierce holes in foil to accommodate leaf stems. When roots are well established, transfer each cutting to a pot.

Or, use coarse sand or a perlite-peat potting mix, and insert the leaf stems into the moist mix. Check for root formation after three or four weeks. If you wish, cover the leaf cuttings and potting medium with a clear plastic bag to help retain the moisture and promote growth. Don't let bag touch leaves.

Light facts

Light is essential to plants. Even the species we admire for thriving in seemingly dark corners need a minimal amount of light to exist. But exactly how much light an individual plant requires is extremely difficult to pinpoint. For one thing, the plants themselves make it hard by breaking so-called rules with abandon.

If other conditions—water, soil, and humidity—are right, a specimen can live under light conditions at variance with the normal. And, fortunately for houseplant enthusiasts, many of the plants show up under two or more categories on listings that divide plants into those that prefer low light, medium light, and strong light. This isn't a fault in the listing, it simply reflects the inherent adaptability of the various species that can live under divergent conditions.

The more you experiment with light levels, the more you'll realize that very few houseplants can tolerate full sun all day. When cultural directions say, "it likes a sunny location," this usually means five hours or less of direct sun daily. By the same token, very few plants will exist in a spot so dark that shadows aren't cast during the day. Most species prefer light levels somewhere in between direct sun and full shade.

Even in the wintertime, it pays to be careful about setting foliage plants next to unshaded windows that face directly into the sun. The reflected light from snow can up the total illumination to the stage where leaves can sunburn. Sheer draperies can minimize this effect, but your safest plan is to move the plants a few feet away from the direct glare.

If too little light, not too much, is your problem, supplement natural light with artificial. Incandescent table lamps, ceiling spotlights, and special grow lamps all create additional "daytime" hours for your unsuspecting plants.

Determined indoor gardeners who wish to use a plant for a major decorative role but find that the location has insufficient light often resort to this trick: they buy two specimens of the plant, and shift the two periodically—one stays for a week in the decorative location, the other in a better light situation. Then, they're switched. This keeps both plants healthy.

If the plants in question are large ones—tubbed palms, monsteras, or dieffenbachias—moving them means work. The best solution is to keep these plants on low platforms equipped with casters. Then, you can roll them from one spot to another with minimum physical exertion.

If you're up to the effort involved, you can move small- and medium-sized plants daily from their usual location in a low-light area to a spot that has brighter light. Leave them in the bright light for at least an hour or two, preferably in the morning

hours. Never, however, actually *sun* a plant that's accustomed to dim light—the leaves will sun-burn quickly, leaving you with an unsightly plant.

Spotting trouble. What happens when a plant gets too little light? Nothing, at first. Plants can survive for long periods on reserve food. Ultimately, however, new growth becomes spindly, new leaves are smaller, and the lower leaves yellow and die. If you have a plant that looks like the bottom specimen in the photo above, you have been keeping it in too dim a spot. Try it in a different location where light is better; it'll soon respond strongly and put out healthy new growth like the vigorous plant at the top.

With too much light, leaves closest to the window will eventually yellow and burn. The plant takes on a slightly faded, unhealthy look. Move it to a spot receiving less light.

Which plant for which exposure? A spot with dim light is far from ideal for plants, but if you must garden under low-light levels, try aspidistra, any of the sansevierias, Chinese evergreen, philodendrons, ficus, palms, dieffenbachia, airplane plant, and English or Swedish ivy. Remember, that even though these plants tolerate dim conditions, they prefer medium light, so don't put them in the dark unless you have no other choice.

In sunny windows (about five hours of sunshine daily), you can grow beautiful geraniums, cactus, and other succulents. Try flowering plants from seed, such as marigolds, or grow miniature roses, citrus trees, or flowering hibiscus.

In the winter when the sun is weaker, move azaleas, impatiens, coleus, and gardenias into this bright light. You must give them extra water in this location or the plants will wilt and leaves will drop.

In the sun, give extra water to any plant in a container that's three inches in diameter or smaller. These little pots dry out quickly, so the plants growing in them need extra care.

In a location that has bright, open light, but little actual sun (usually called medium light), the sky's the limit on what plants you can grow successfully. Almost any foliage plant will do well with these light conditions, and quite a few species will flower here if given the spots closest to the windows.

Glossary of terms

Aerial root. A root that grows out from the stem above the soil level.

Bloom. In addition to the common meaning of a flower, this word is also used to describe a whitish substance on the leaves and stems of a plant, which rubs off on handling.

Bract. A leaflike part associated with flowers and sometimes inaccurately called a petal, as in the poinsettia.

Bud. The portion of a plant from which a shoot, cluster of leaves, or a flower develops.

Bulb. An enlarged underground bud that develops roots and sends up stems, leaves, and flowers.

Compost. Organic matter made up of fermented or decomposed materials, such as leaves and grass.

Compound leaf. A leaf divided into two or more leaflets with a common leafstalk.

Crown. Point at or just below soil surface where stem and root join.

Cultivar. A species or variety bred in cultivation.

Cut back. To cut or pinch off growth at tips of plants to encourage development of side growth.

Dormant. The rest period of a plant or bulb during which growth ceases or slows down.

Established plant. Plant that is well enough rooted to take hold and thrive without extraordinary care.

Flats. Shallow boxes that are used for growing seedlings.

Force. To make a plant bloom before its natural season of flowering.

Frond. The leaflike part of a fern. Often also applied to the compound leaves of palms.

Fruit. The mature seed of a plant.

Germination. The first growth that's observable in a seed.

Graft. The shoot or bud of one plant that is merged with another. The fused plant that continues to grow is also called a graft.

Habit. The shape or growth form of a plant, such as a trailing habit or a vining habit.

Humus. The decomposed organic material that is capable of holding large amounts of plant nutrients and moisture. Usually added to a garden soil and sand to make a potting mixture.

Hybrid. A cross between two or more plants of different parentages.

Internode. The section of a plant stem between two nodes or joints.

Leach. To wash minerals and other soluble matter from soil by watering.

Leaflet. One of the divisions of a compound leaf. Also a young leaf that's not fully mature.

Leggy. Said of a plant that is tall, does not branch as it should, and often has no leaves except at its top. The condition usually is caused by lack of pinching back at the proper stage of growth, or by too little light.

Lobe. Portion of a petal or leaf that divides the whole to the point about at its middle.

Midrib. The main rib of a leaf, which is a continuation of the leafstalk.

Mildew. Fungus that attacks plants, especially those exposed to lingering damp conditions. Appears as furry, whitish coating or discoloration.

Mist. To use a fine spray of water on foliage of plants.

Node. Point on stem from which a leaf or bud arises.

Offset. A short side shoot that is used for propagation.

Photosynthesis. The action of sunlight on chlorophyll of plants that results in food formation.

Pinch back. See **Cut back.**

Propagate. To increase plants by such methods as division, cuttings, air layering, or from seed.

Rootbound. When roots completely fill a pot. The soil ball is a mass of entwined roots.

Runners. Thin, wiry shoots that some plants send out, which produce new plants at their ends.

Shard. Pieces of broken pottery or items such as bottle caps that are placed over the hole in the bottom of a pot to ensure necessary drainage, yet keep soil from washing out.

Slip. A stem cutting taken from an established plant for the purpose of propagating a new plant.

Spathe. A leaflike structure that encloses a flower cluster.

Standard potting soil. All-purpose potting soil that is sold commercially in garden centers and nurseries.

Sterilization. Treatment of soil to destroy organisms in it.

Syringe. To wash a plant by means of a fine spray of water.

Tamp. To lightly firm down fresh soil with the hands or a flat utensil.

Tendril. The slender prolongation of a leaf or stem that clings to a support as it grows.

Transpiration. The giving off of moisture through the pores of leaves.

Transplant. To remove a plant from the place where it is growing and move to new location or container.

Tuber. Swollen underground stem that bears eyes.

Variegated. Including more than one color. Having a dappled appearance.

Variety. A subdivision of a species.

Whorl. A group of three or more leaves or flowers appearing in a circle at one node.

Index